She Persisted

ONE HUNDRED MONOLOGUES FROM PLAYS BY WOMEN OVER FORTY

She Persisted

ONE HUNDRED MONOLOGUES FROM PLAYS BY WOMEN OVER FORTY

PREFACE BY JACQUELYN REINGOLD

INTRODUCTION BY THERESA REBECK

EDITED BY LAWRENCE HARBISON

THEATRE & CINEMA BOOKS

Guilford, Connecticut

Applause Theatre and Cinema Books
An imprint of Globe Pequot, the trade division of The Rowman & Littlefield
Publishing Group, Inc.
4501 Forbes Blvd., Ste. 200
Lanham, MD 20706
www.rowman.com

Distributed by NATIONAL BOOK NETWORK

British Library Cataloguing in Publication Information Available

Library of Congress Cataloging-in-Publication Data

Names: Harbison, Lawrence, editor. | Reingold, Jacquelyn, writer of
  preface. | Rebeck, Theresa, writer of introduction.
Title: She persisted : one hundred monologues from plays by women over
  forty / edited by Lawrence Harbison ; preface by Jacquelyn Reingold ;
  introduction by Theresa Rebeck.
Description: Guilford, Connecticut : Applause, [2021] | Series: Applause
  acting series | Summary: "A collection of monologues from plays by women
  over forty" —Provided by publisher.
Identifiers: LCCN 2021040477 (print) | LCCN 2021040478 (ebook) | ISBN
  9781493061310 (paperback) | ISBN 9781493061327 (epub)
Subjects: LCSH: Monologues. | American drama—Women authors. | American
  drama—21st century | Acting—Problems, exercises, etc. | LCGFT:
  Monologues (Drama)
Classification: LCC PN2080 .S476 2021 (print) | LCC PN2080 (ebook) | DDC
  808.82/45—dc23
LC record available at https://lccn.loc.gov/2021040477
LC ebook record available at https://lccn.loc.gov/2021040478

CONTENTS

PREFACE

On June 5, 2018, Brooke Berman posted on Facebook "WARNING. RANT . . . Composing an Op-Ed in my mind about the generation of female playwrights sandwiched between the Baby Boomers and the Pussy Grabs generation. Because I fear we will be forgotten."

Within hours there were forty pages filled with four hundred comments. "It's true." "OH MY GOD YES." "a sandwiched generation." "submerged writers." "Now that young female playwrights are paid attention to, we're told we're old." "We were told to pay our dues and hopefully we'd earn a place at the table. THEN THEY MOVED THE FUCKING TABLE."

Playwrights were named. "You are on the list." Everyone had their favorites. "You are on the list." Women in their 40s, 50s, 60s. "You are on the list." Pages of names. "You are on the list." I was on the list. But what good was being on a list of the soon-to-be forgotten? What if we did something to get those playwrights and their plays into—theaters?

Theresa Rebeck invited some of us to her house. We ate, drank, and wailed. We felt better, but we still weren't getting produced. Months later, after noticing a highly touted list of women/nonbinary playwrights barely included us, Susan Miller invited more of us to her place. We ate and drank, but instead of just wailing, we began to . . . organize. We kept meeting. And organizing. We no longer ate and drank at meetings, since, thanks to Yvette Heyliger, we were now at the Dramatists Guild, where we focused on actions. We formed an Executive Committee: Cynthia Cooper, Cheryl Davis, Yvette Heyliger, Olga Humphrey, Jacquelyn Reingold, Sarah Tuft, Lucy Wang. We wrote, and rewrote (hey, we're writers) our mission statement:

Honor Roll! is an advocacy and action group of women+ playwrights over forty—and our allies—whose goal is our inclusion in theater. The term "women+" refers to a spectrum of gender identification that includes women, non-binary identifiers, and trans. We are the generation excluded at the outset of our careers because of sexism, now overlooked because of ageism. We celebrate diversity in theater, and work to call attention to the negative impact of age discrimination alongside gender, race, ethnicity, faith, socioeconomic status, disability, and sexual orientation in the American Theater, and beyond.

We are, at the time of this writing, thirteen hundred members and growing.

Some of us started writing plays later in life, and though early in career, we're excluded from emerging writer programs. Some of us landed productions while young but learned if we weren't famous by forty, theaters closed their doors. Some of us found more success in TV, fiction, film, teaching. Some of us were waylaid by mentors who savaged our plays, while others were traumatized when those mentors sexually harassed us. Some of us, in addition to sexism, faced racism and homophobia. Lately, most of us delight in cheering on our younger sisters who are, finally, getting productions, but we puzzle over theaters that consistently confuse "fresh voices" with "young voices." All of us know the odds are against us getting produced by high-profile theaters, but we keep doing what we love: writing plays.

Honor Roll! is a grassroots group of self-initiated actions. Sarah Tuft helms a campaign to redefine "Emerging/Early Career" to include women who are forty plus. Claudia Catania, Cindy Cooper, and I have a program to feature members in "Playing on Air" podcast recordings. Betsy Howie and Catherine Castellani host our monthly NYC Happy Hour. Yvette Heyliger wrote a personal essay for *The Dramatist Blog*. Kathy Anderson, Liz Amadio, and Betsy Howie compiled extensive statistical research. Stephanie Alison Walker created a portal for members interested in TV. Jacqueline E. Lawton, Lucy Wang, Winter Miller, and Sarah Tuft honed our language to reflect intersectionality. Jacqueline Goldfinger started a play reading exchange via NPX. Bayla Travis organized a Musical Theatre Panel. Barbara Kahn, Jean Hartley Sidden, and Saviana Stanescu all planned theater events. To name just *some* of our actions.

This book began, full circle, with a post on the Honor Roll! Facebook page on November 7, 2019, about publishing our short plays and monologues. It wasn't a rant. It was an action. I contacted prominent theater editor Lawrence Harbison and pitched the idea over a New York diner breakfast. His face lit up. Not only was he enthused, he persuaded John Cerullo, the head of Applause Theatre and Cinema Books, to publish two books, one of ten-minute plays and one of monologues. Larry edited and selected the work, while the Publishing Committee

(Suzanne Bradbeer, Cheryl Davis, Lucy Wang, and I), worked tirelessly on our end. It was way harder than we ever imagined. Yet worth it. It is a thrill to introduce the Honor Roll!'s first books. I hope there will be many more. Thank you to the Publishing Committee, the Executive Committee, Lawrence Harbison, John Cerullo, Theresa Rebeck, and most of all, to the no longer forgotten, submerged, or sandwiched playwrights in Honor Roll! Now, we need to see productions of these writers *onstage*.

Jacquelyn Reingold
Playwright and founding member of Honor Roll!
June 1, 2020

INTRODUCTION

Years and years ago, when I was a young playwright who happened to be a woman, I was issued plenty of warnings about what that might end up looking like. One of my teachers, who positioned himself as my mentor, thought I was really talented but he told me I needed to be careful not to let myself get "ghettoized" as a woman playwright. Idealistic and passionate (and did I mention young?) I replied: It's a great thing to be a woman playwright! It's a new world! They are waiting to hear from us! We share the planet! People want to receive our stories!

It turned out to be a little more complicated than that.

Few people thought of the appearance of female playwrights as a "Wow! We haven't heard from the women!" kind of moment. It was a deeply painful time, even a terrifying time, to be a woman playwright. It was like you were being deselected even before they'd read your play. There were many different ways to explain why theaters were not interested in producing plays written by women, but none of them were, I'm sorry to say, very persuasive. The primary reason being thrown around was that our plays were just "not good enough." If you got anyone to explain what "not good enough" meant, they gave you nothing, really. It was like the idea that a woman had written this made it bad before you even got past the set description. Female playwrights were trapped in kindergarten, also known as the underground reading series, for far too long, while frankly a lot of guys who were actually "not good enough" got handed the keys to the kingdom.

That went on for quite a long time. And it's not as if people didn't know this was happening. Allies—often, powerful male allies—told us to rethink our names, to go by our initials, to use a male pseudonym. The problem, it seemed, was the gendered name, right there on the title page. If you could somehow scrub that gender out of the name of the playwright, you'd have a much better shot at a fair read. This move had already led to a sea change in orchestra auditions: Once the auditions were held behind screens, so that no one could see the gender of the auditioner, orchestras went from being utterly lopsided, in terms of gender representation, to being pretty much evenly balanced. The theater just needed to somehow figure that bit out. So concerned friends everywhere tried to kindly explain to us: Equalize the playing field. Make yourself a man.

If you pointed out that this was appalling and that women are every bit as good as men, and our stories are just as important, and what's more the planet hadn't really heard them yet, you were branded as "difficult."

If you tried to point out that playwrights are supposed to be "difficult," well, you see where this is going.

There was seemingly something essentially wrong with the idea of a Woman Playwright. Women are not supposed to speak up like that. If you're going to write a play it should be more like an Emily Dickinson poem. Women who wrote plays unfortunately seemed too loud by definition. If you were a woman writing about what you knew—women's lives—that meant you had a "feminist agenda." Which was bad, even though men were at the same time being wildly celebrated for having misogynist agendas.

This wasn't that long ago. It was much more recent than it should have been. Still, it went on for a long, long time and frankly it was ridiculous.

And then we rose up.

In 2002, the great Susan Jonas was our John the Baptist, with Suzanne Bennett spearheading and publishing a powerful NYSCA Report which went into damning detail about how female creatives in the theater had been systemically discriminated against for decades. In the 90s, we discovered, there were fewer new plays on Broadway than there had been in the 1920s. We were going backwards. Julia Jordan, Sarah Schulman, and New Dramatists held a town hall, inviting artistic directors to come and explain why their programming systematically excluded women directors and playwrights. That got covered by the press, and slowly but surely this ridiculous situation was observed and acknowledged. Opportunities for women started to appear, a small trickle and then a small stream. The numbers—which were being tracked by the Dramatists Guild—started to change. More plays by women were being produced, and there was more than one woman playwright at a time.

Sadly, we were still excluded from the awards season, so we started our own awards, The Lillys. And then the Kilroys were born, an organization which put together lists of wonderful new plays by female playwrights, so that artistic directors who wanted to know where those plays were had a place to look. The Guerrilla Girls stepped up and left messages *everywhere* about the importance of women artists and audiences. (Women make up about seventy-five percent of our audience, which is partially why we can't figure out why this wasn't addressed years ago.)

And then #Me Too happened. And another shocking window opened, revealing the systemic discrimination against women in show business. The focus of #MeToo very much centered on the sexual abuse of women in the workplace, and how impossible it was for women to find a legal remedy to predatory and bullying behavior from men in power. But alongside that, women knew there were other behaviors that went hand in glove with sexual abuse. Women were still being excluded or suppressed in the corporate boys' clubs behind the scenes, and women's writing was not being promoted or included in the front lines of storytelling in television and film, as well as in the theater.

The NYSCA Report. The Guerrilla Girls. The Lillys. The Kilroys. #MeToo. We are moving ahead. Progress has been made.

And yet. There were many plays written during those decades of struggle. We're not there yet, and the plays are being written still. Women are not yet seen as full partners in this mighty enterprise, the theater. And yet plays are being written. We still have a long way to go. And plays are being written.

And they're being written by many of the same writers who fought through all those years to be heard. These women are in their forties and fifties and sixties, and they have been writing a long time, and they are at the height of their craft. These are tight, complex, nuanced pieces of writing which no one has seen because for too long they weren't looking.

These are important writers, and important plays.

History has not yet caught up or even had the thought that maybe we should go take a look at those plays that stand as witnesses to human nature and joy and suffering, which tell the story of women fighting for the rights of all women storytellers to be heard. It's time to look at what was silenced, during those years of lost writing. The plays are still here, because all these women persisted.

Theresa Rebeck
Playwright
May 19, 2020

EDITOR'S NOTE

This volume contains one hundred monologues for both women and men from plays by some of our finest women playwrights, who happen to be over forty. It is my hope that it will help to combat the rampant ageism which pervades the theater.

Although the age of the character is given in each monologue, many may be done by actors of any age.

Lawrence Harbison

110 STORIES
Sarah Tuft

Dramatic
MITCHELL PERITZ, 44

MITCHELL PERITZ (PEH-ritz), *a chiropractor and body worker who volunteered at the World Trade Center site after 9/11, confronts the reality of the ironworkers' overworked bodies. He speaks to the audience.*

MITCHELL   Oh yeah, the ironworkers. Holy Shit. It's sort of like working on petrified wood, these guys are so muscular. God, it's probably my second morning there, this guy was just thick, you know? He had no neck. His head was screwed into his shoulders. No wrists. Just fingers sticking out, like Popeye. So, he was huge. Nice guy. Says, "Look, I can't move my arm." And he can't. I say, "Are you kidding me? I'd need a chisel to get into that thing!" He's laughing. He had a good ol' time. So, after a whole series of testing, it looks like it's his intercostal muscle. I'm screwed. There's no way I'm getting through to this guy's intercostal muscle above his pec. So I did a lot of tissue work on his neck and upper traps. Then I actually went into the pec muscle itself. I let this guy know I was in his chest! So he got like, eighty to ninety percent of his movement back and went on his way. Another one came in with a fucked-up shoulder. I said, "Are you out of your mind? You want me to fix a fucked-up shoulder you've been using for years in fifteen, twenty minutes? No problem. Let me just get into a phone booth. I'll put on my cape."

110 STORIES
Sarah Tuft

Dramatic
BOLIVAR ARELLANO, 56, Ecuadorian American

BOLIVAR ARELLANO (BOWL-i-var ar-e-YA-no), *a staff photographer for the* New York Post, *rushed down to photograph the 9/11 attacks, only to encounter the trauma of seeing people jump from the Towers. He speaks to the audience.*

BOLIVAR   My name is Bolivar Arellano. For the last thirty-eight years, I am a press photographer. I photograph civil wars in Colombia and Nicaragua and a lot of shootings and massacres in Ecuador, you know, people killed by the paramilitaries. I don't like injustice so I use my camera as a weapon. My camera is my machine gun. Because in El Salvador, the military shoot people and they say, "Oh-oh, we didn't shoot the bodies. We just shoot the air." But I made it show that they are liars because the paper published my picture shooting the bodies. So, to stay there, I would be dead. I have to move here. I thought I saw everything until the World Trade Center. Yeah. That day was Election Day so I shoot all of the candidates. And I was developing the pictures when my photo editor come in, "Bolivar, hurry up. There's a crash, accident, a plane!" So, I took my car. And I passed like, forty red lights and in about twenty minutes, I was right there under the two buildings. I start taking pictures. And I saw the first one. I saw him jump from the building. Then I saw when he touched the ground. No. His body was in pieces. It was dismembered. So uh, the other eleven that jumped, I didn't want to see them touching the ground. So, I take only the pictures looking up. And that is going to be forever in my mind because I was praying, you know, in my mind. I was praying, "Please, please God. You want to take them? Take them. But don't let

3

them touch the ground. Please give them wings." You know because the beliefs of the Catholics is that God not only hears you pray, but that God reads your mind. So that was what I was praying, you know, in silence and . . . but . . . he didn't listen to me.

110 STORIES
Sarah Tuft

Dramatic
JIM SNYDER, M.D., 36

DR. JIM SNYDER, *a child psychiatrist volunteering at the World Trade Center site after 9/11, struggles with the disconnect of discovering comfort in the middle of a disaster area. He speaks to the audience.*

DR. SNYDER   There was this Starbucks so near the Towers, its windows had been blown out, ash had been literally blown into the store—powder all over the tables and chairs. When I first peeked in, I saw a bunch of firemen and policemen and MTA workers having coffee. There were cakes and pastries laid out and behind the bar, the espresso bar, was this police sergeant. So I go in. I just wanna grab a cup of coffee but the cop yells out, "Cappuccino?" I think, "Well, this is a little awkward." You know—I'm in the middle of a tragedy and I'm about to order a cappuccino. In a bombed-out Starbucks. Very surreal. So I say, "Well if that's no problem . . ." And he whips up this unbelievable cappuccino! I say, "You should work here." And he says, "This is my passion!" And he pulls down his sweater and—now this is a police sergeant—he has a gold chain on and dangling from the chain are three gold coffee beans. So I say, "This man knows and loves his coffee!" At first, I had trouble with this whole scenario. I thought, you know, is this right? Should they be doing this? But by the time I left, I thought, "Absolutely!" Because here are people risking their lives, doing things beyond what we had ever thought we'd need to do. We're in New York City and yet we're in a war zone, smoke and debris and buildings falling and thousands of people dead and here's this one little nugget area where you can get a cappuccino made by a police officer. And I thought, "God Bless. This is beautiful thing."

110 STORIES
Sarah Tuft

Dramatic
TONY ESOLA, 33

TONY ESOLA, *an ironworker (Local 483) from New Jersey volunteering at the World Trade Center after 9/11, found Pepsi cans from ironworkers who put up the building whose wreckage he's dismantling. He speaks to the audience.*

TONY   I love the heights. I love heights. The higher the better. I don't mind hanging out on top of a beam like, I'll take lunch up there. The steel beams on the Trade Center—it's a hollow square, like that . . . hollow in the middle. The funny thing is, I've found so many cans—old beer and soda cans—of when they first built it, with rolled pop-tops. Not a scratch on them! Everything in that building is totally pulverized, but these old cans are coming out like new. Guess as they drank them, they put them down the access which is hollow. So, when you're cutting a beam, a can rolls out and you're like, "Oh—a Pepsi can from the sixties." So, I have four or five cans so far. I have one beer can that—instead of using a can opener to open it, they used a spud wrench. And a spud wrench is something we use. It has a wrench on one end—it's long—and it has a point on the other end. You know, some ironworker from back in the sixties opened the can—and that ironworker was putting the building up—and here I am, an ironworker taking it down, which is kind of like, "Wow." Just seems like a window in time—the beer can, with the hole in it, from the spud wrench. Back then you could drink on the job.

THE AGENCY
Laura Rohrman

Dramatic
ANNE, 20s

ANNE has gotten a job working as an intern at the oldest literary agency in New York City. In a matter of weeks, she's transformed the place. Everyone in the office is either in love with her or jealous of her. Her true motivations for wanting to work there have never been stated. Here, she tells her secret dreams, but no one hears her, because everyone who sees her doesn't really see her.

ANNE   Stop laughing. I have dreams you know. And I'm young still. Do I have to give up my dreams so soon? Once I had a vision to feel more ambition, but that went down in flames. I had so many ideas, but no one encouraged me. I was good at acting and my acting teacher in high school confirmed that I wasn't very special or something like that. She gave me a small part in the school play and when I complained about it, because I deserved a better part, she said something about me being average. But you had to audition to get into her class and I made that cut, but then I never pursued acting after that. But then in college, when I was study-ing French, some actor friends were talking about a play. I decided to audition and it happened: I got the lead part. And the character was sleazy. She slept with all these men. I played her with aplomb, of course. I wore a negligee for the entire show. We got a standing ovation and I kept hearing the audience roars in my head. It was amazing. I loved . . . the attention, the adulation. I was no longer ordinary. I could do anything. But then I went to France and instead I started to dance but even then, there was something I still wanted to say. There was a story in my head and it wasn't dead, it grew with vibrancy by the day. I sat in a Parisian café drinking latte after latte and I smoked many cigarettes. I even wore a writing cap. I wrote a play . . . There's more to me than a pretty face. That's why I'm here. It's not to sneak and find an acting job for myself. I could care less about that. It's because I want to be a writer!

ALL ME, ALL THE TIME
Susan Cinoman

Dramatic
JAKE, late 40s

After the kids have graduated from high school, physician JAKE decides it's time to start the new life that he's been waiting to launch for years. In this play about two couples on the verge of divorce, JAKE explains himself to his wife, SHARON.

JAKE   I've had a long night. I've been driving for hours. Sitting in the front seat of that car, thinking. Taylor in the back. I didn't even know what to say to her. Taylor, she had those amazing curls, didn't she? I have images of her running to the door when I went to the hospital. She must've jumped out of her bed by four to get down to the door before I left. I didn't pick her up, Sharon. Kissed her on the head, that's all. I had rounds. What could I do? I was the one who had to steer the ship, didn't I? I don't think I've had a conversation with Taylor for ten years. And the sad thing is, Sharon, I really don't want to. It's terrible not to like your own child. I mean, I love her. But I just don't know if I like her. I'm sorry. I'm horribly sorry about all the rest of it. I'm sorry about Taylor. I'm sorry about us. I'm sorry I . . . wanted things to be a whole different picture. I didn't go into this thinking it would end. Who would ever go into something beautiful and exciting and thinking it could ever end? But it does end somehow. And then . . . you get someone else in your bloodstream, and that's it. You just . . . you just let yourself go . . . you give yourself that first injection. Of her. Of her need for you and her interest in you. It's intoxicating in a way that you've never been drunk in your life. And, then that's it. It's over. And I'm gone. I tried. I tried to live in the past with you, Sharon. I tried to think of those times in the beginning, but I couldn't.

I couldn't remember when we first stopped talking to each other, when we stopped making love—did I want you and you didn't want me—and I was so angry that I didn't want you back, or was it the other way around. Who fell out of love with who? I tried to untangle all of that. And I couldn't! But you can't just keep giving the past your thoughts and your attention and your love and your hate. You give all that and the past gives you back nothing. It's the most one-sided relationship imaginable, the one you have with the past. The past is so selfish. When do we stop trying to be us in the past and become Sharon and Jake?

APOLOGIES TO VIETNAM
C.S. Hanson

Seriocomic
MISTER, 30s

MISTER *is a grad student working on a PhD in Cultural Anthropology. He speaks to* KAI, *the proprietress and waitress of a small café.*

MISTER   I'll level with you. Level with you means "be really really honest." It's my advisor. Says my dissertation lacks authenticity. What a prick. Says I gotta make it more real, whatever that means. Okay, I admit, there are all sorts of burgeoning immigrant populations right in my back yard, and I thought I'd take a look at the Vietnamese. I need something slightly obscure. The Chinese, well, they're everywhere. The Vietnamese, more rare. I've studied my history. And done research like a madman. And watched every Vietnam movie ever made. But I've never really talked to any of you people . . . That didn't come out right. Look, I need to make my dissertation sing with a local color. I've gotta bring my advisor pages—reams of paper—filled with . . . won't you tell me your story? I need to know your story. Are you happy here? Seriously, living here, working here? The Lower East Side, this city—what's it like for you? What was that phrase you said before? Ko-ko something or other? . . . No more questions. Let me just say, your eyes are remarkable. Tell me if I'm on the right track here. You don't have to say anything. Just nod if this makes sense. I picture people floating down calm bodies of water, surrounded by water lilies, with rice paddies in the distance. (*Pause.*) I've never done anything like this before . . . but I want to apologize for the U.S. involvement in Vietnam. I have to get this off my chest. It was not right to kill innocent men and women and children. Would you allow me, on behalf of, well, the people of the United States, to apologize to you, to your family and friends and loved ones, to all of Vietnam? It was wrong. I wasn't there, but I know it was oh-so wrong, and I, well, can I hug you? . . . I have gone far beyond my intentions. Understand, I came down here to gather some clues, some insight. But, hey, I won't say another word.

APPLE COVE
Lynn Rosen

Seriocomic
ALAN, 20s

ALAN, *who works at a sporting goods store, is caught by his wife,*
EDIE, *sleeping in their baby crib hugging a stuffed animal. She has
been trying to get* ALAN *out of the crib so he can go to work. He's
clearly at his wit's end, his mind and mouth are racing.* DUKE, *whom*
ALAN *references, is a mysterious new security guard at the Cove
whom* ALAN *senses* EDIE *is attracted to.*

ALAN No! I can't, Edie. I can't go out there! Out there jiggly.
Here. Home. You and me—safe. Good. Outside house jiggly.
Ride to work? Risky! Honk. Beep. Finger! And that's just in the
Cove. Blurs on the highway. Threats! Threats everywhere. Job
nice, this here, that there. But the people, *the people*! Jiggly!
Employees, customers itch for a slight, a fight. I miss the nuns
at St. Magdalene's. So strict. So knowable. This one customer,
did I tell you? Massive arms. Reptiles, riddles, tattoos covered
his body. A white guy. Or a black guy. But why do I say that
when he was also red, and blue, and green? Like an animal. A
toucan! Words all over him. Asian, Arab, Hebrew. I'm guess-
ing. It's all a guess! All those mysteries in one man. There
are billions of men, times oh say three mysteries per man.
Edie! Imagine what's out there that we don't know about!
We must be careful. Even here in our beloved house, in our
protected Cove, things seep in. That crazy wild rose in your
garden. Where did that come from? That Duke! Things go
wrong. We were leaving here, Mom and Pop and I, when it
happened. In a blink. Around a bend. Before it was homes.
When it was all swamp and lagoon. The truck drove toward
us, the fish sloshed in the cooler, then they were gone. And
I was lost, so lost. Life is so fragile, Edie. Tragedy lurks below.

I won't let it happen again! I won't let it happen to us! I'm on alert now. We'll both be on alert in our little world where all is familiar and safe. Like the pot holder with its friendly scald. Or the toaster with its curly cord (*Panicking.*) that connects to a wire outside, which leads to a power grid in Pensacola, that connects us to the world—Edie, get rid of the toaster!

THE APPRAISAL
Jeanne Dorsey

Dramatic
SONIA, 80s

SONIA, *a slightly tipsy woman, has agreed to sell her "perfect seven" Greenwich Village penthouse. Here, she is addressing her real estate broker.*

SONIA   You're recoiling from the past?! How can you when it's what you're selling? That's what this is! This home, the sale of which will make you a whopping commission, this is the past! It's my entire life and it's about to disappear. Do you know what that means? You can't begin to imagine. I can tell you a few things but they'd barely scratch the surface. I can tell you that not only is this the scene of my miserable, beautiful, stupid, wild devouring marriage, it's where I nursed my daughter, curled her hair, made her Halloween costumes, read to her, sang to her. It's where I read and wrote long letters, cooked, celebrated, tolerated, loved, cared, despised, laughed, raged, kissed, hit and got hit, spat, hugged, fucked, screamed, relaxed, suffered, talked, drank, argued and loved some more. It's where finally I nursed my crazy, overbearing, dying husband and where Naomi and I sat shivah and where I realized that as hard as I tried I was never a very good mother to her. She's my despair and my joy. I so wish she were here with me. I'd trade a million exquisite Prague teapots for that privilege. That teapot was the end result of our fight in Prague by the way. He told me . . . Jesus . . . he told me . . . he told me that I never should have married him, that I should have stuck with making art, that I was much better at that than I was as a wife or mother. I got into a hot bath and sobbed. He came back to our hotel two hours later with his sad little face and an exquisitely wrapped box containing the teapot. I accepted it as an olive branch even though I wanted to smash it over his head. The truth is I was far too tasteful, bourgeois and scared to do any such thing. So, on we went with our life together. No woman should have to put up with that kind of talk from a man. Now there's a quaint notion. Would that such a choice "to not put up with" were possible in my generation. In my day, we women put up with it. And sweetheart, I've had it good compared to most women then and now. I've had it better than most. But I've learned never to underestimate misogyny. It's in the water we humans drink. If you have a shred of doubt about that remember who's sitting in the Oval Office. That this country could elect a rancid pile of white male narcissistic scum over a brilliant accomplished woman tells you something about the world we continue to live in. I'm ashamed that I had such hope this time.

BAD DAUGHTER
Julie Weinberg

Dramatic
LILY, 60s

LILY's husband has cancer and she tries to get her alienated daughter's help to convince her father to do chemotherapy.

LILY Why are you so cruel? You know what, you don't have to love me—or even like me. You have to help your father. And don't tell me how to deal with your father. I've been married to that man for many years. (*Beat.*) I can't stand it—I just can't. I don't know how anybody does this. It's unbearable. I know you hate me, but you love him—I know you do. I know you want him to do that chemo. Please, talk to him. (*Beat.*) I don't know where to sleep. Your father's down here. I can't lie upstairs all alone.

Come upstairs and say goodnight to me? I said goodnight to you every night. You used to fall out of your bed. I used to sit there and wait for you to roll out of your bed but I'd fall asleep and then it would happen anyway so I gave up trying to stop you and I just put a big comforter on the floor. And then Daddy would go in and wrap it around you. You seemed to like the floor. I don't know why.

CALLIE'S TALLY
Betsy Howie

Dramatic
THE WOMAN, late 30s

THE WOMAN *speaks to her sleeping infant daughter in hopes of being forgiven for a series of emotional meltdowns.*

THE WOMAN   I'm so sorry, baby girl. Please don't wake up. I know I have been short with you in the last few days. I have not handled your crying in a way of which I can be proud. I'm just praying I haven't screwed you up too completely yet. You're such a good baby. You deserve a stressless mama. I am feeling very much on my own these days and you are getting the short stick on that deal. With a father and a grandma all within arm's reach, we are the last two folks on earth that should be alone. But Grandma's still trying to get settled and your father . . . well, he returned home from Chicago last night and I immediately told him that we had to come up with a new plan between us, a more equal sharing of time with you. He said he completely "gets it" and will give me no argument. Then he outlined his schedule for the next several days and, of course, he can't be here. He reminded me that he had told me of all these important lunches and meetings several weeks ago. To that, I wanted to say to him: I'm in Babyland! Do you honestly think that telling me two weeks in advance that you are going to a luncheon and that you have a meeting will register as back-to-back events which are coming on the tail of five days in Chicago?! Have you ever been in Babyland? There are no calendars and you are not legally allowed to look more than three minutes into the future. There is no self and anything that smacks of the outside world doesn't register without incessant repetition. But I didn't, because of my vow to never have a fight in front of you. And, of course, he has not been in Babyland. And that is the whole point. I'm afraid that's just the way men are. Daddy's brain doesn't work like ours. I heard it from Oprah. You see your brain has two sides and they handle very different kinds of jobs. In order to be fully functioning, information must travel back and forth between the two lobes. In women, the connective tissue between the two lobes is substantial—like an eight-lane super highway with high-speed bullet trains running alongside. Men have an old path run through a cornfield. It's not that your father is self-centered, it's just that he is unable to handle more than one thought at a time. He starts with himself and he is such a big subject that he never gets to the next one. So, since we know that the connective tissue issue will never allow him to multitask, we must take another approach. We must get your father to start with you and get to himself second. Because, as we know, baby girl, you are the very biggest subject there is. There's no getting over you.

CALLIE'S TALLY
Betsy Howie

Dramatic
WOMAN, 30s

The WOMAN *tells her mother her concerns about having a baby with a man who is significantly older than she is.*

WOMAN   He's fifty-seven, Mom! That's a problem for me. And it's a hard one because I find I get mad at him for being fifty-seven, and it's not his fault. He's always been very consistent chronologically. He hasn't changed. But everything else has and fifty-seven is really old to be having someone who is zero. Don't you think so? Don't you agree? He could be a wonderful dad. He's very smart. He's very good with his students. You know how charming he can be and he looks really good in fine clothing. The thing is, I like our life. I like our house and our cats, the work we do and the fun we have. But Mom! It's all about to change. Forever. Sometimes, I see it all, how it lies before me—and I know I'm going to die. Not now, but I will and that's really upsetting because I don't want to die. Even when I'm feeling like one lonely raw nerve ending, I want more. I don't understand why we get invited to this party if we're not going to be allowed to stay. I want to stay and I want to dance all night. This is no great leap from the baby question, you know. You can't help but recognize that having a baby is as much a giant step toward the cliff's edge as burying your grandmother. Maybe even more—because now it's not just a case of one less person in front of you to block your way—now there's actually someone behind you who could decide to push. I don't want to be pushed or fall or leap. I just really don't want to go. I want to stay at the party.

CALLIE'S TALLY

Betsy Howie

Dramatic
WOMAN, 30s

The WOMAN *is speaking to her newborn baby, expressing her concerns about how her life has changed and what the future may hold.*

WOMAN   I just weep. I'll sit with you in my arms and you are gazing up at me, or something close to me, it's hard to tell where you're focused. But this peace sits so softly upon your face that I begin to weep. I do not make noise because I do not want your father or your grandmother to hear me because this is not postpartum depression and it's not the baby-blues. Tears are not streaming down my face because of the fear that I feel which I do or the anxiousness that I feel which I do—the tears are from a place somewhere outside of me that recognizes sheer beauty and absolute trust when it sees it. Those that watch from that place recognize when something too good and too pure and too soft has landed among us and the watchers send tears to fall from whatever pair of eyes gaze most nearly upon that sweetness. So, it appears, I'm being transformed by the tiniest of people. You have wrecked me, destroyed my perfect frank glibness. And you threaten to rob me of my desire to care about any number of things—work, play, money. And so, what is the billable cost of that? How do I charge you for stealing my want to do anything but stare at you? If you have nicked my desire to care about cash and career then how can I care enough to want to charge you for the theft? Perhaps I will return to my senses by spring and understand again that this is a fair and equitable deal and it's important that I teach you the value of things. So, I will continue to total the tally on the chance that one day I will see some part of my sense again. On the chance that, one day, you will open up your lovely little long-fingered hands and let me take just a peek at my soul which, it would appear, you now own. Pardon me for rambling, but I'm just recovering from being split like an amoeba.

THE CHAOS TRADE
T. Cat Ford

Dramatic
JOEY, 30s

JOEY meets with Diane Simes, the Head of Human Resources for Brakeman and Dyre, an investment bank, who is handing out severance packages and cardboard boxes to each employee she fires.

JOEY Take the package and the numbers. Hey, why do they call it a package anyway? You don't have to answer that. I was musing. Musing is good. I mean how about musing about being here for five years, making the firm tons o'moolah and then getting a lousy "package." What is my "package" anyway? Two weeks' pay for every year of my life in the esteemed position as a trader plus vacation pay? Great! Super! That's a good trade. Now I know why I'm getting the axe and Rafael is still toiling away. He's got more weeks coming. Been here what? Thirty years? Ten weeks of severance versus sixty. Good. Good. That's very good. Very efficient. Two and a half months' pay versus fifteen. Very bottom line. I'm proud of you. That's how to make decisions. It's not about who is best long term. This is about short-term bottom line. Live to fight another day, right? Then you can hire another smart asshole like me for less, right? Right? When I joined this place, I had ideals. I thought it was a true meritocracy. A land where if you worked your butt off and were clever you could make it big time. If you did the best, you won! And that was all that mattered. No right, no wrong—just winning. A way of life, right? A nice way of life. Survival of the fittest. Civilized! And now . . . now . . . FUCK!!!!!!!!!!!!!! I'm confused. What's going on? I'm the fittest! I've been doing things right! I've been making money! I made this firm over twenty million dollars for two years running. I am still making money! Today! Today! When everything is going down the shit hole—my trades—trades I was told to close by cheese for brains in the corner office—trades which I did not close—are the only trades alive in this entire stinking institution! My strategy is working and yet, yet—I'm the one being spit out! Spit out due to short- term thinking rather than long-term analysis. Spit out due to someone else's mistake? I repeat—I'm making money. Isn't that what we're supposed to do here? Isn't that what we make? Money? You, me, Rumplestiltskin? What happened? Why are you firing the best producer on the floor? My life ends with two weeks for every year I've given this place? Do you think that's a fair trade? Is it? I don't know. I really don't know. Sounds like a short to me, even with the vacation pay. And, by the way, just so you know, for the record, I want to be clear—I never took a vacation. Oooooops! Forgot about that! I loved this place too much. How crazy is that? This was my stupid life. I loved it. How many people feel that about their work? How many? Do you feel that way about this . . . this . . . We had the American dream by the tail, but it turned out to be the tail end didn't it? The saddest—the stupidest—the saddest thing is I thought, get this, I thought I actually made a difference. I thought I mattered to this place. What a hoot! What an idiot! What happens now?

CHESS AND THE MIDDLE EAST
Martha Patterson

Comic
QUEENIE, 30s

QUEENIE *interrupts an Arab and a Jew playing chess together in the park who are having a dispute over how the problems of the Middle East should be solved.*

QUEENIE   Excuse me. I was sitting over there on a bench on my day off, listening to you two old coots play chess and bicker about Palestine, and let me tell you, women know very well how to draw a line down the middle. Think the French were arrogant to give each side half, do you? Listen. My husband's a Frenchie and he's a good lover and he respects me and that's what matters. And drawing a line down the middle of Palestine makes sense. Oh, I know some of the land's worthless for growing things. But folks can *live* on it, can't they? Jews and Arabs have to find a way to share. As in housework. I trained my Frenchie husband to do half. He makes the beds, takes out the trash, even cooks three times a week. A real Escoffier and a gentleman. And women know how to draw the line down the middle in bed, too. He and I sleep together but it's only "intimate" if we both agree to it. No funny business, no sexual assault. I don't want any randy old husband of mine taking advantage of my good nature. Like I said, my husband's a real gent. That's what I have to say about drawing a line down the middle. Ask any woman. Now just stop arguing and get back to your game. Better yet, why don't you rent roller skates at the pavilion over there and while away an hour on wheels? Might be fun and solve your problem. I'll leave you alone now.

(She exits.)

CHICKEN AND THE EGG

Dana Leslie Goldstein

Seriocomic
CARA, late 20s

CARA, a biologist, has come back to New York from California for her grandparents' fiftieth anniversary. She hasn't been home in a while, and her grandfather—a holocaust survivor—is now living in the woods behind their large family estate. He has been sighted, but no one can make him emerge. The family is afraid he won't come out in time for the large anniversary party that's been planned for him and his wife. CARA, who has always been close to her grandfather, but hasn't seen him in some time, thinks she can succeed where the others have failed.

CARA Grandpa? Grandpa, is that you? I know I don't have to tell you how much I missed you. But I did. Like a lot. Grandma's right. I can feel you out there. I like it. I feel watched over. Like the whole place is under your protection. Let me see you, Grandpa. I won't tell. I won't tell anyone about those tunnels we dug either. I bet that's where you've been sleeping. Hey, I—I brought you a copy of my new paper. In German. Do you believe that? It got translated into German. Maybe some long-lost relative over there'll read it and not even know they're related to me. Just some research paper by some crazy American biologist. You wouldn't think it was crazy, though, Grandpa. You'd understand. Even if chickens aren't mammals. It's relevant, I know it is. More than the kangaroos. Something happens when the chick's still in the egg, before it hatches. It's been birthed, it's escaped its mother, but it hasn't emerged yet, so it's in this, this limbo, you know? Born, but not born. And while it's like that, it has this power—*diapause*, it's called—to stop everything . . . and heal. Like, if the mother hen gets off the egg so the temperature drops, the chick can sense that, and it stops developing. Or if the eggshell cracks a little, the chick stops growing, while the shell repairs itself. It's amazing. I've got my lab set up so I can study dozens of eggs at a time. In different stages. I wish you could see it. I have to force myself to go to sleep because I don't want to miss anything. It was hard to leave it in California and come back here. Thing is, I'm pretty sure *we* can do it too. I can't prove it yet. We just . . . we have to find that place. That limbo—where regeneration can happen. Call it home base, the drawing board, the egg, whatever, but then anything's possible. Do you see? Grandpa? You can start all over again. We all can. Is that what you're doing in there? Trying to—regenerate? Pause? Heal? I get it. I really do. You aren't even there, are you? I'm just talking to myself. Good thing no one's out here. I'd really look like an idiot.

CHILD SOLDIER
J. Thalia Cunningham

Dramatic
DESTINY, 18, African

DESTINY's *dead child has appeared to her in a dream.*

DESTINY   I do love you. My beautiful baby. I'm starting to
remember what happened. Do you? You were only a few
months old. But already such a bright little girl! Laughing
and chattering such pretty sounds. How I loved you! I would
have gladly given my life for you, but it wouldn't have
helped. It was time to go out fighting again. They gave us
drugs, slitting our foreheads with razors so cocaine would go
directly into the bloodstream. Then they performed the ritu-
al to make us brave. There you were, the next one to be sac-
rificed. He picked you up. I screamed and cried, but he held
his knife to my throat and said he'd kill me, too, if I made one
more sound. He slit your throat while a soldier about my age
held a cup to collect your blood. The cup was passed around
for all of us to drink. I drank without thinking. My eyes were
only on you, as you slowly stopped crying and wiggling and
breathing, the last drops of blood dripping out your chubby
little neck like water from a leaky tap. Then you were still, so
still. Your blood ringed my lips as I rushed forth to gather you
in my arms, but they wouldn't even let me hold you once
more. The knife was a sudden flash of unbearable pain. Your
flesh was on fire, but then, I saw you slowly going to sleep.
To join the land of the ancestors. His knife was in my back as
we carried our guns out into the bush. I turned back to look
at your little body, a naked scrap of promise lying in the dust.
He prodded me, forcing me to turn around, mixing your
blood with mine. The scar is all I have left of you.

CIRCLE GAME
Julie Weinberg

Dramatic
HARRIET, 20s

HARRIET *is in a club in Tribeca (New York City) with her best friend,* DEE, *who wants to leave with a guy she met.*

HARRIET   Why can't we go out and be just us? I want you to hang out with me—just me.

Why can't you do that? You're fucked up and I'm fucked up for not telling you you're fucked up. What the hell happened to the truth? Jesus Christ—we both know that tomorrow morning you're going to wake up in some cockroach invested hole on the lower Eastside and I'm going to get the five a.m. phone call. You'll be crying and freaked out and guilty that you had blackout sex with this asshole and that you abandoned me on my big night—our big night—and then I'm supposed to comfort you. I love you Dee, you're my best friend but you've got to choose right now. (*Beat.*)

If you want to go with this fucking bartender to Danceteria— go. But know this—if you go, I'm done. This'll be our last night out together ever again.

CLEARING
Barbara Blatner

Dramatic
JIM, 20s

In Clearing, KIRT *shot and killed his best friend* JIM *during a Taliban ambush in the Hindu Kush Mountains while serving in Afghanistan.* JIM's *ghost appears and talks to* KIRT.

JIM   'Member how you found me, after you saved the day like a true hero, killin' those bad Talis? Wind lappin' at my legs, chest streamin'. You and everyone thought the towelheads killed me in the battle. You forgot you did it, man. I don't really blame ya, but I wanna tell ya, I was comin' back to fight by your side, I was. Don't be mad anymore, bro? We did that blood thing as kids, got the Apache strength in us, 'member? Or that day I swum out at the picnic into that concrete pond, I was six, my little heart thrashin' hard. I almost drowned, but I *needed* that water, in my arms, my mouth. Everyone was laughin' when you pulled me out coughin' up my gullet, like I done somethin' wrong that was gonna *stay* wrong. But *you* knew I was just a pure idiot swimmin' out there, innocent as the day I was born, even if I got the rottenest timin' in the whole world. Just sometimes you *need* something, you *do* somethin' 'cause you *need* it. Your mother needed a buddy, bro, we were buddies a while, that's all, that's the truth. You're still my people, ok? You'll always be my people, my family, you and Lisbet. Don't be mad anymore. You'd still let me come home with you if I wasn't . . . bro? One more thing. You're killin' Talis like crazy, I'm fadin' under that awful moon, and I hear it, like you always say: Everythin's breathin' togeth-er! The big Hindu mountains, birds, insects, moon, breathin' in out in out, like one big cell, like you always say. That's all, bro, that's all.

CYCLONE AND THE PIG-FACED LADY

Dana Leslie Goldstein

Comic
PETERSON, 40s–50s

PETERSON, *a comic book publisher, has had it with his star creator,*
SALLY KAPLAN, *who hasn't produced anything for almost a year.*
SALLY *finally has sent him her latest work, in which she kills off her*
lead character (and money-maker), the glamorous gypsy super-
hero "Cyclone." Exasperated, PETERSON *has shown up at* SALLY's
apartment.

PETERSON   "The Death of Cyclone?" What the fuck are you
trying to do to me, Kaplan? This is career suicide, that's what
this is. Unless this is maybe another cliffhanger? Okay, so
here's where I've got the problem. It's with the dying part.
It sucks. I waited a year for this? Okay, okay, let's take a step
back here. I didn't tell you what I like. I like the babies. Always
have. Tiny, little premature babies in the incubators. High
stakes. Freaky, right up your alley. But you gotta let her save
'em. Nobody wants to see tiny little babies fried to a crisp.
Do what I pay you to do. Send her in. Let her save the babies.
Or I'm putting somebody else on the franchise. People been
telling me since the beginning this was too much for you. I
should just let you draw it, and have somebody else do the
story. But I always defended you. No, I said, Kaplan works
alone. That's her genius. She doesn't need anybody else. But
maybe . . . maybe they were right. Maybe it's time I put somebody else on the character. I don't want to, but you know
what you signed. I could name fourteen guys right now who
want your job. Three of 'em work for me. One of 'em's almost
good enough. And he's already got some half-decent ideas.
Like how about finally giving her a real costume? Don't make
me do something I don't want to do. Look, sometimes you

39

get a happy ending, especially at an amusement park. It's good for people. Let Cyclone save the day. But you know where the rights are. You wanna walk, that's fine. I'm so generous, I'll let you take the Pig-Faced Lady with you, but Cyclone stays with me. At least she's got a future. Cyclone stays. And she stays alive. She's so friggin' sexy, she can't die. But the pig . . . She's an assault on the eyes. I'm happy to cut my losses. Keep the hottie, lose the pig. It'll be good for business. What's it gonna be, Kaplan? I know, I know. You're about to say: "I can't separate them. They're two sides of the same—whatever-the-fuck." If I had a psychiatrist on my pay-roll, I might have time for that shit. I'm gonna say this once. Make her the hero, Kaplan, or it's over. Today.

DAUGHTERS OF THE SEXUAL REVOLUTION
Dana Leslie Goldstein

Dramatic
JEFFREY, 30s–40s

JEFFREY, *a psychiatrist, tries to convince his wife,* NINA, *to give their marriage another chance. They've just hosted an ill-fated dinner party, and the last guests have left. The time is 1976.*

JEFFREY   When you came back in, that glow in your cheeks—I thought—it reminded me . . . When you used to dance—You were dancing the first time I saw you. Your cheeks looked like that. It was on the plaza after—a march or—I was coming off a shift, and there was a bonfire. You let me dance with you. Remember? (*Pause.*) We haven't danced in . . . I knew it would be you from the moment I saw you. I could picture . . . our future. I used to think I was the luckiest man in the world. We could be that way again. I'm not sorry they left. I'll move my things back into our room. Tonight. That will help. I know it will. We can fix this. I know there's a way to fix this. Nina. If I . . . If I've pushed you . . . you know I'm only trying to do what I think is right. For you. With the valium. It seemed like it was working. For a time. You were happier. More peaceful. You don't remember what you were like. You don't remember any of it. I was there. I watched you falling apart. Experimenting. That night you banged on my door. You couldn't stop shaking. But you knew exactly where to go. And who to go to. *You* came to *me.* You knew how I felt about you, and you came to me. You were right. I gave you exactly what you needed. I made it all slow down. I took you away. Changed your life. Look at all this. I made all of it possible. I made Ricky possible. Think about it rationally. This is what marriage is. You wanted that. I know what *I* want. I'm very clear on it. I want to sleep in our bedroom tonight. I want to have another child. I want to be happy, some of the time at least. I don't think that's so much to ask in a marriage. Is it, Nina? Is it? You can't even look at me. Look at me! (*Softer, almost hypnotically.*) This was all a misunderstanding. You *should* stop taking the valium. You shouldn't be on it if we're trying to have another child.

DAUGHTERS OF THE SEXUAL REVOLUTION
Dana Leslie Goldstein

Seriocomic
JEFFREY, 30s–40s

*JEFFREY, a psychiatrist, is trying to make a good impression at a
cocktail party with new neighbors.*

JEFFREY   Not all politicians are crooks. At least not in this
country. This may not be a popular sentiment, but it's my
belief that temperament is to blame. We all want our leaders,
our politicians, to be charismatic, exciting, larger than life,
but there's a downside. Big personas lead to big choices, big
fears to big paranoia. Their missteps reverberate. But they
don't have to. I personally believe that if Richard Nixon had
been on anti-anxiety medication—they're extremely effec-
tive now—he never would have gotten himself involved
with those criminals at all! Nixon's own insecurity was his
worst enemy. If he'd had some valium, he'd still be in office.
This country doesn't need more religion; it needs more *legal*
pharmacology. With the right prescription, Nixon might
not have felt the need to tape anyone. Would've been more
comfortable with himself. And then we—you, me, the
country—wouldn't have had to go through all that. Think of
the ramifications. We'd be less cynical. About everything. I
am, of course, biased. But I've been prescribing more valium
than they can keep on the shelves. The results are indisput-
able. And that's just for your regular folks, your housewives
and bus drivers. When a figure in power is able to keep his
head on straight, well, you get the open door with China,
Détente, you get out of Viet Nam—but with honor. And
then, when it's time for reelection, you get calm. No
unhinging of the moral compass. (*Beat.*) I should write a
book about it.

DOING SCHOOL
Carol S. Lashof

Dramatic
FRAN, 20s

FRAN *is a first year English teacher at a large public high school. She has accused a student of plagiarism, perhaps wrongly, and a senior colleague has questioned her judgment and her fairness.*

FRAN   Test scores. Class participation. Attendance records. Maybe those are "superficial attributes," but what else do you go on? When a student has racked up so many absences you almost have to fail them on that basis alone, doesn't that tell you something about their "motivation for quality work"? And I don't know why they're absent. I've got kids who are absent because their parents took them out of school to ski in the Alps for a week, and I've got kids who are absent because their best friend was killed in a drive by, and they had to go to court to testify. Or they're absent because their grandma died, or their dog died. Or they're too damned busy getting stoned to give a—to bother with coming to class. But it doesn't matter anyway. All we're allowed to consider is whether the attendance sheet comes back from the office marked "excused" or "unexcused." And most of Will's absences are unexcused. He was absent for peer editing day. I'm supposed to teach the writing process. It's built into the syllabus: brainstorming exercises, rough drafts, peer review, revision. And if a student fails to do any of that? And then out of the blue, he turns in a polished essay. Using vocabulary and concepts we've never even discussed in class: "dissociation," "derealization," "depersonalization." Wouldn't you be suspicious? Wouldn't you think something was wrong?

DO I HAVE TO?
Felice Locker

Dramatic
JANE, late 30s–early 40s.

JANE *is physically disabled. She has mobility issues and uses some kind of mobility device.* JANE *is speaking to Momma Eagle, a magical being and an eagle, when she sees that the container that held all her belongings is now empty.*

JANE   It's gone. It's all gone! There is nothing. My life was in there. My life's work. All I collected and all I curated! The memories I protected and the lives I rescued from time and weather and destruction and bad people and poison . . . I moved them all into this big box that I set down right here for safekeeping in this place big and broad enough to hold it safely in this home on the range Colorado. All is gone. The container is empty. Empty like a stomach never fed. My cooking utensils and milliner's tools and shoe making molds, and ladders and saws and scythes and rakes, and seamstress and tailor tools and pharmacists' cabinets and workbenches, and chopping bowls and butcher block tables and lanterns and hammers and. Hollow in my ears, my heart racing rising I can't control the pounding drum in my chest. Pin marks and impressions and stains and dents and cuts and rubs and ridges and cracks and sweat and tears and, and blood and blood and blood. Like I'm blindfolded and my friends, lovers, family stand out of reach. I can't touch them. I can't see. My head's like a bomb exploding, exploding the memory of before it all went up in pieces and pushed away another time and place. Life collected and contained. I came all this way to protect my everything. Just an empty box—An empty box crushed and useless like I am. Am I alive? Nothing holding nothing having nothing being nothing. I am nothing on top of nothing on top of never and nowhere and no how. No Jane. Not Jane. No. No.

ELEVATOR INTENTIONS
Shellen Lubin

Dramatic
HE, 20–40, African American

The speaker is actually a fantasy in the mind of a white woman on an elevator with an African-American man who didn't push a button when he got on the elevator.

HE   Look, I'm sorry. I'm sorry that you're here on this elevator alone with me. I'm sorry that I'm not still in my suit from work, so you can't tell I'm really a nice middle-class respectable nigger. I'm even sorry if you've had a lousy day. 'Cause I've had one fuckin' lousy day, too, if it's any of your goddamn business. I lost a major client this afternoon. And when I went home hoping to cool out, my cat had broken my stereo so I couldn't even listen to any music. So, I called up my buddy, Al, who lives on the fity-third floor here—maybe you know him—Alan Kay—53C—and I asked him if he wanted to have some company. "I'll come over to your neighborhood," I said. "I don't mind. I'll get there when it's still nice and light so I don't freak out all the white ladies who know they don't recognize me as one of their doormen or delivery 'boys.'"

And I'll take a cab home—if I can get one—so they don't have to cross the street when they feel me walking behind them, or roll up their car windows when their BMWs get too close to me at a stoplight." But the subway broke down on the way up here, and I sat in that hot, stinking car for an hour, which is why I didn't get here 'til "a little before eight" and ended up on this elevator with you and your goddamn anxieties. And don't think I can't feel them—I smell them, I breathe them in—I can't get away from them. I'm trapped in here with you just as much as you are with me. So, keep your fucking imagination to yourself. Where do you think you get off trying to figure out who I am, trying to decide whether or not I'm worthy to share this space with you? What do I owe you? Why the hell do I have to prove myself to you?

EXTREME WHETHER
Karen Malpede

Dramatic
JOHN, 60s

JOHN *is a world-renowned climate scientist.* REBECCA, *30s, is his colleague, now lover. It is the summer of 2012 and it is as if time and no time has passed. Here, he shares his fears with* REBECCA.

JOHN   We must stop putting ourselves at the center of the universe, as if what we knew mattered, as if we could figure things out. Oh, I realize how impossible that is for ego-driven creatures like us. What difference can we possibly make? You or I, to what happens here? Yet we persist in believing once we know the truth we can control results. When, in fact, our intelligence has been the ruin of us. Human beings are responsible for global warming. Our ingenuity has brought us here. But, Rebecca, I hesitate even to say this out loud. This is the conclusion I've reached: events have flipped out of our control, no, not just control, natural events are now far beyond our ability to know. That's what your catastrophic ice melt is telling us, along with the tornadoes, hurricanes, droughts, fires, and the sea level rise. The causes and effects we thought we understood, the clever models we built, have become obsolete. We have reached the tipping point. Now. This summer of 2012. Whether we wish to know the truth or not is of absolutely no significance any more. Intelligence might have worked in our favor ten or twenty years ago, when we first understood. Willful blindness might have been harmful last year. But what happens next will be completely outside the realm of human understanding. We can no longer predict because all of the systems we have studied so carefully over the years, all our graphs and the charts, our satellites, the models, observations, the theories no longer reflect anything but a world that has vanished on our watch. The systems we came to rely upon no longer exist. The human brain can no longer comprehend because human kind is no longer at the center of anything except the chaos human kind has caused.

FACE IT
Julie Weinberg

Seriocomic
ELIZA KLINE, claims to be mid-40s

A contestant on Face It *can win up to 100k in plastic surgery and relaunch a failing career. Today* ELIZA KLINE, *fallen Soap Opera diva, has to make her on-camera confessional and reckon with her humiliating fall from stardom, when her career stumbled to a halt on the L.A. set of* All Our Tomorrows.

ELIZA   Okay, I'm on All Our Tomorrows for maybe a year and then the show moves from New York to L.A. Everyone says be careful, Hollywood is a moody mistress. She can flip on you in a heartbeat, but I don't see it. I'm playing evil Nikki London and her alter-ego sweet Nora, split personalities in the biggest hit show on daytime. We're getting all the ratings. Emmy shoo-in—why not? Hollywood—it's a show-biz dream bubble. The hawks fly over my glorious mansion in the canyon. And okay, maybe I'm lonely. Maybe . . . (*Beat.*) But hell, I'm fine—what am I saying? I'm a fucking star. My agent's on cloud nine. My mother acts like I just gave birth to Baby Jesus. (*Beat.*) Fast forward four years later and we're shooting the big scene, the weekend before Nikki's sentencing for the murder of disgusting Uncle Tommy. I'm out on bail staring into a beautiful stone fireplace. Then, out of the blue, the director says, "Throw little Lambie"—that's my stuffed lamb and dual personality trigger—"Throw Lambie into the fire." I'm stunned, but I do it—and the whole cottage goes up in flames! Out of the smoke my mother appears and drags me out onto the driveway.

(*Babbles as* Nikki.)

"Where's Nora? Where's my sister? I've killed her too. My face, it burns, everything hurts, it hurts." Then I disappear into the night in an ambulance.

(*Calms herself.*)

I have to say, that was some of my best work and incinerating Lambie—that took everything out of me. I'm out sick for a week—one week—And what happens? I am *fired*. Me, who single-handedly took the show ratings through the roof, and I get no help, no love, no gratitude. The moody mistress flips the hell out. Fired. But the worst part: How do I find out? By watching it on TV!

FATHER'S DAY
Yvette Heyliger

Dramatic
LEW, 38, African American

Victim becomes perpetrator when an estranged husband and father abuses his daughter. This is direct address to the audience.

LEW Oh, God! What have I done? What have I done? I couldn't help myself! God help me, I couldn't help myself! She is so beautiful. She smells so sweet. Her skin is so soft. And those little breasts with the sweet little nipples. Her hair so long and pretty and that cute little figure . . . I just got carried away! It's been a long time since I touched anyone or was touched by anyone. I couldn't help myself! I wanted to be touched, needed to be touched! I know she was nervous. I know that she was. You're supposed to be on your first time. But I was gentle. I didn't want her to be afraid. Never! I love Vanessa! I love her so much. She's my little girl. I would never hurt her. I would never force myself on her. That's like rape and I'm no rapist! I'm her father. I didn't do anything wrong. Kids have a natural curiosity at this age. I'm just trying to exploit it—I mean, explain it, you know, so some young punk doesn't take advantage. Hey! Don't you look at me like that, like I've crossed some line! You think you're so different from me, well, you're not! I'm seeing the same things out here you are. I'm not the one peddling half naked young girls with their parted lips, full breasts, and begging eyes up on bill-boards and in magazines and on the TV, am I?! Am I? I mean, how's a red-blooded American man supposed to react to that? I'll show you how!

(He grabs his crotch.)

You got nothing on me; you hear me? Nothing! I didn't do anything wrong! I love my daughter. I carry her picture in my wallet like fathers do, who love their children. She's Daddy's little princess.

A FIELD GUIDE TO THE AMAZON
Phoebe Eaton

Dramatic
JULIET LIDDELL, 18

After attempting suicide by overdose, JULIET LIDDELL *jerks the chain of her mom's paralegal Habiba Mahmud by threatening to go AWOL from the hospital.*

JULIET   Listen, this Hermès blanket my Mom gave me? Because she's like overcompensating or unbelievably clueless or thinks I'm a horse and I told her not to but she didn't listen as per usual? It finally got ripped off over here at the like, correctional facility and it's like ridiculously over-air-conditioned and there's like this stupid sadistic concentration-campy blanket allowance. Dr. Jeffries is not gonna talk to you. He's not allowed to discuss me with you. It's like, completely against regulations. He basically shows up once a day and it's always at the end and it's too freeze-your-ass-off even for him. He's some Alzheim-y old beardo who needs to get on home before CSI starts and his cream of chicken soup gets cold. Listen, shit gets ripped off at hospitals all the fucking time. There's no locks in a psych ward! And it's not like, the other inmates. It's the staff. The fucking staff!

Who wants to work in a hospital? The money sucks and it's boring and disgusting and you can get attacked with like, staplers, because people are genuinely off their rockers and if I tell anybody something's wrong—any little, the slightest nothing anything—the whole entire desk gangs up on you like you're some traitor to their mind-blowing incompetence. By law they have to call the police and file a report. It's a whole thing, a giant hassle, and they all hate you 'cause it means tossing the cells it really is like jail only everyone knows it's somebody on staff and that gets them extra pissy 'cause it's this big steaming pile of extra work for nothing! That these dickheads can't even admit to. Which is why I'm so bailing. I'm packing all my shit right now. Yeah. I refused their stupid meds this morning that turn you into a floppy stuffed animal who wouldn't feel a blanket being swiped and who knows what. My birthday was in April and like, the California Bar Association's Empress Dowager of Efficiency never got around to filing for guardianship because I am so the last thing she even thinks about when she pops an Ambien and crawls into bed at night with a vibrator and the Law Journal. So, the answer is, I can totally man-overboard because I am a fucking adult now under the law. The last seventy-two hours I'm on record as no longer a danger to myself. I can totally be one-hundred percent gone girl in like fifteen minutes from now, and no one will be able to find me.

FLESH AND BLOOD
Annie LaRussa

Dramatic
RUTH, 40s

RUTH *is married to* WILLIAM/BILLIE JEAN, *who is a banker and a cross-dresser.*

RUTH   I don't think I love you any more, William. That's why I'm sad . . . When you . . . became Billie Jean. I tolerated Billie Jean but . . . I miss William. I loved William. And because I loved William, I tolerated Billie Jean. I wanted to make you, my William, happy and so I helped you discover who you really were, inside and outside . . . a her. That made me so happy . . . for a while, but not anymore. I am so sorry Billie Jean but I really . . . I really don't like you. I don't like the way you've taken over my life. I don't like the way you take up all the closet space. I can't stand wet nylons hanging all over the bathroom. I am sick of you using my mascara. Hate that you leave fake nails everywhere. And my perfume . . . that is MY scent, not yours, you can't just take my perfume and wear my smell. It took me a long time to find that scent, and it's MINE, you can't just steal it. I don't want Billie Jean smelling like me. I HATE that you smell like me and you don't smell like William anymore!! I liked the way William smelled. And I feel kind of lonely without William. We go out now and it's never simple . . . you in your high heels and me in my flats. We can't just walk down the street holding hands. And although I am so proud of you, the staring gets overwhelming sometimes for me. I know I can't let the haters win but this is a battle I wasn't prepared to fight. You have been preparing for it for years. You put on your armor of designer dresses and makeup and fake boobs and you feel powerful. I follow behind, underdressed and pale. I think I need some time away from you. I think I need some time, Billie Jean . . . I think I need some time, William. I love William, and because I love William, I am leaving you, Billie Jean. Go live your life . . . in happiness.

FREEDOM SUMMER
Cynthia Grace Robinson

Dramatic
NORA, late 20s, African American (passing for white)

August 1964. On her wedding day, NORA *must defend her decision to abandon her black identity to her sister,* CARRIE, *a Freedom Rider.*

NORA   You see a reflection of yourself, and the reflection says that you are colored. And you see a reflection of me, Nora, and the image in that mirror says that Nora is white. Mirrors don't lie, Carrie. They are pure truth. They're a reflection of what *is*, not what we want things to be. Look at my skin. It's as white as any white woman you've ever seen in your life. It's as white as the skin of that woman mama's been working for the past twenty years. When I walk down the streets of Beacon Hill, white folks look at me and smile. They see what's in this reflection. They're not afraid, they don't feel threatened and they don't think they're better than me. I move through this world with my head up. White men tip their hats and open doors, white women say "good afternoon" and compliment me on my hair or my dress or my purse. I can go anywhere I want and feel safe. I can enter a department store and try on a hat, or a dress, or shoes and no one even blinks an eye. No one thinks I'm dirty, no one thinks I'm going to steal, no one questions my morals, everyone assumes I have enough money to pay, and they often extend me credit. They all assume I'm well-bred and that I know right from wrong. When I go to a restaurant I can sit where I want and when I order my lunch, I receive service with a pleasant smile. I go to work dressed in a suit, not a uniform. I work in an office and I sit at a desk. I don't have to clean that office bathroom or scrub that office floor. I get to sit where everyone can see me, in front of a typewriter all day, answering phones. No one expects me to pick up their mess, or take care of their children, or cook their meals, or wash their stinking clothes. You have no idea how easy this skin makes my life. You will never be able to comprehend how glorious this is. That's my reality. This skin is my reality. It's safety. It's my pass to having the life that I've always wanted, that I've always dreamed about, and I wouldn't give it up for you, or mama, or daddy, and certainly not for any so-called "movement." I wouldn't give it up for anything or anyone in this world.

GETTING IN TOUCH WITH YOUR DARK SIDE
Laura Rohrman

Comic
MARY-ANNE 30s

MARY-ANNE's friends have taken her away for the weekend as an intervention to get her to stop obsessing about her ex-boyfriend, DAN. She drinks a special drink that will let her get all her anger out. This is a few minutes after she's had "the drink."

MARY-ANNE   Well, after he cheated on me I just couldn't believe that he ever said that he loved me . . . you know? He wasn't even good in bed. Do you know that he used to always beg for me to suck his dick but he'd never do the same for me . . . I mean what an asshole. I'm so pissed about all the times I . . .

you know . . . and then he said that I was stalking HIM. And he told my friends. THAT FUCKING ASSHOLE. I . . . just. Look how I feel about Dan . . . I don't even care about him okay. He can go fuck his whore, what do I care. (*Beat.*) I hate you Dan George . . . I hate your small dick! I HATE YOUR SMALL DICK, DAN! YOU MOTHERFUCKER. YOU ARE GOING TO DIE. I'LL KILL YOU WITH MY BARE HANDS AND EAT YOU. Ah.!!!!!!!!!!!!!!!!!!!!!! ASSHOLE!!!!!!!!!! DAN!!!!!!!!!!!!!! DIE MOTHERFUCKER DIE. (*Beat.*) That's not the half of it, actually. I'M GOING TO CUT YOUR HEART OUT OF YOUR CHEST WITH MY FUCKING TOOTH-BRUSH ... Yeah, yeah, yeah . . . OHHHHHH!!!!!

(She starts to have an orgasm standing up. It will go something like this.)

Uh, uh . . . uh . . . yes, YES, YES . . . oh yeah . . . not you . . . this is . . . uh, uh AHHHHHHHHHHHHHHHHHHHHHH.YAHHHHHHHHHH-HHHHHHHHHHHHHHH.

GHOSTS OF BOGOTÁ

Diana Burbano

Dramatic
LOLA, 30s

In the Grand Cathedral, Bogota, Colombia, LOLA *eulogizes her grandfather, who has finally died after clinging to life for way too long.*

LOLA   Hola!! My name is Lola and I am an . . . well clearly, alcohol, drugs, sex, etc., etc. Everything to excess or why bother, right?! This won't take long. I know most of you, though if I'm honest it's mostly from accidentally friending you on Facebook. Anyway. Who's actually mourning this motherfucker? Raise your hands.

(She counts.)

Oh my god. Put your hands down. Seriously? Ok. Raise your hands if the old fella fondled you when you were little.

(Waits.)

Hmmm. So just the two "Americans?" No one else? Cool cool cool. You shouldn't lie in church. I don't know why Saúl felt compelled to use my body or my sister's body. I've been talking about it so long that the idea has lost its bite. Yes, I was molested, but so was, I don't know, EVERY other woman in here? I mean. All of us? And we all turn a blind eye and let him do what he did, and I honestly can't figure out why, or if anyone said to him stop, or if you all just sighed and figured it was inevitable. I turn that over and over in my head. The mundanity of it. The casual use of my body. Her body. Our bodies. Nothing but holes and mounds and weakness and lies. The biggest lie, and the one that makes my bones ache, is that our lives as women are worth nothing. Our history's erased. Our lives forgotten. I'm here to tell you that we are

EVERYTHING. Goddesses of creation, motherfuckers! This body creates life, multitasks like nobody's business, is a hella great writer, and can hold me up here, even as it's full of cancer and death. Full of cancer like him. But unlike him, I'm not afraid to die.

(*She raises her fist.*)

Here's to the old man! Celebrated not at all in life. Un-mourned in death. Bury his shit in the deep dark and let the worms crawl as they may. Hit it Jesus!

GIN AND BITTERS
Susan Cinoman

Dramatic
Naomi, 35

NAOMI *and* TOMMY *are best friends, but* TOMMY's *gay, and* NAOMI's *in love with him. Their friendship is confused by the week they spent together years ago in Paris, in bed. Finally,* NAOMI *thinks she's found a way to break away from her unrequited love.*

NAOMI The other night, when you were off on one of those "excursions" that neither of us talks about to each other . . . something did happen to me, I guess. I was in the middle of my typical waking fantasy about us at your Mother's in Somerton. Did I ever tell you this one? Oh, it's good. See, we're at your Mother's and she's just finished making for you all of your favorite white food. Mashed potatoes, vanilla pudding, and creamed corn, and there are you and me, sitting at her kitchen table laughing, and making contemptuous faces behind your brother's back, when suddenly you get up and you say, "Everyone . . . I have an announcement to make. I love Naomi. I have always loved her and I'm going to marry her once and for all." And just about then the phone rang and shook me out of my daydream and it was Len Steinman's assistant giving me the address of this party in New York. I thought, "I'll go. I'll do something that would show you . . . really show you. Someone wanted me, so you should, too." But at this party . . . it was so strange. It scared me, Tommy. I saw all of these sort of magical people glowing and floating like ectoplasm around the room. And I thought about Len years ago, this sweet guy I'd treated like some kind of sad eunuch. How many guys like that were there? Guys who didn't know about *Susan Hayward* or *The Imitation of Life.* And suddenly this young man Mark! He's standing there right in front of me. He was the most glowing figure of all. A messenger. And although he didn't have little wings on his ankles, he did have something. Now I know he reminded me of you ten years ago. All full of promise and possibility. But at the time I became aware from the minute I had gotten to the party . . . I had no thoughts about my fantasy of the white food and the wedding announcement, which was something that I, a perfectly capable person, right, which I have desperately longed for . . . for an embarrassingly long time. I realized since the moment I had gotten to that party in New York I didn't have a single thought, Tommy, about you.

GO DOWN, MOSES
Dana Leslie Goldstein

Dramatic
ALBERT BECKER, 40s–50s, African American

Against his better judgment, DEAN ALBERT BECKER tries to persuade the students to vote the way he, and the university administration, want them to, on whether or not to fund bringing a controversial speaker to campus.

BECKER Excuse me, Everyone. I see we have a larger turn out than usual. If you'll allow me, I'd like to take a few moments before the voting begins. I am faculty advisor, but this is your organization. Your Student Assembly. Still—As many of you know, I am a veteran of the civil rights movement. The central aim of that movement was to raise up a particular people, but we didn't stand for division. We weren't trying to lift one people at the expense of another. What I remember most clearly from that period were the bridges we built. I was born in Michigan, went to college there, had never been farther South than Washington, D.C., when I joined the Student Nonviolent Coordinating Committee. I couldn't have been much more different from the Mississippi sharecroppers we were registering to vote, except for the color of my skin. And I couldn't have been much more different from my oldest friend—the friend I made during that summer, when it was a death-defying act just to register to vote. To vote! He was a Jewish refugee from World War II, a veteran, a generation older than myself. But we walked dusty roads together from house to weather-beaten old house, trying to convince people to go down to the court and sign their names to a voting roll. Even though that meant they could lose their jobs, their homes, or worse.

We lived in fear together when Goodman and Chaney and Schwerner went missing, mounting fear that didn't subside when they were found, dead, that didn't subside when they were mourned by the nation, that didn't subside even when we returned to the North, in safety, while all those Mississippi friends we'd made had to stay and continue to fight. We chose to come here, to this Quaker college, with its long history of peaceful resistance to inequality. I wanted to be part of that legacy. A legacy of bridges. If Mr. Farrakhan insults Jews to raise up Blacks, he is not part of that legacy. If he divides human beings from each other, he is not part of that legacy. If he calls Hitler a great leader, regardless of *any* other brilliant and uplifting things he says, he is not part of that legacy. I would never take away anyone's vote. I know what it cost to win that right—but I urge you to use that vote, and use it wisely. Vote against funding this lecture. Thank you.

GO DOWN, MOSES
Dana Leslie Goldstein

Dramatic
ANGELA CARTER, 20–21. African American

ANGELA *was instrumental in bringing a controversial speaker to her small campus. This led to a protest and an unwanted visit from the nearby KKK. She now regrets her actions. She admits this to her Ethics professor and mentor.* BECKER *is the Dean of Students.*

ANGELA   None of this would've happened if I hadn't suggested him. I pushed, and I made speeches. I . . . I should've known . . . I did know. That they might show up. The KKK. They were right next door. But I thought it would be the way you said. They'd stand. Peacefully. When I played it out in my mind, no one got hurt. But the hypocrites, they'd see—who they were standing *with*. I thought he was a coward. Becker. A mouthpiece for the administration. I couldn't understand how you were friends. But he defended Farrakhan. He stood up to the Klan. "I disapprove of what you say, but I will defend to the death your right to say it." Becker really did that. I completely misjudged him. I remember feeling so free the first time I heard Farrakhan. That's what I was trying to recreate—but it wasn't like that at all. "A consoler of men"—that's what he said black women needed to be. It's just a different kind of box. That's not the message I thought he'd bring. You don't know how they're all looking at me now—I need to take responsibility. Isn't that the ethical thing to do? People got hurt. Not just Katie. I brought him here so he'd step through those gates and burst this bubble. But those animals came too. Is that what happens when the gates come down? I practically invited them in. And now there are people in the hospital. Because of me. Why should I be allowed to come back to class when they can't? I never should've come here in the first place. I loved your class. You made me think. And question. And maybe even teach someday. The way he made me feel when I was a kid—I felt that in your class. But I can't stay. Here. I can't put this behind me. No one here will ever let me put this behind me.

GOOD MOURNING, AMERICA

Lucy Wang

Dramatic
YOUNG SOLDIER, late teen–early 20s

*Ten days after the terrorists' attack on September 11, 2001. A
YOUNG SOLDIER, ready to fight the terrorists and report to base,
looks for an empty seat on an Amtrak train. No one will make room
for him.*

YOUNG SOLDIER   I ain't afraid of no stinking Osama Bin Laden.
We gonna kick his Fucking Muslim ass. Blow his fucking ass
to Mars. I ain't fucking afraid of nobody. Truth is I'm looking forward to it. Yeah, I am. Born a fighter, I'll die a fighter.
I know war is serious business. Why the fuck you think me
and the guys are drinking as much as we can before we get
there? As I told that old man who told me to shut the fuck
up, hey old man, relax, you want your social security check,
well, I'm gonna secure it for you. How's that grandpa? Save
you from governmental failure to issue. The least you can
do for me is let me have my last hurrah. To cheer me on. It's
like that polka song, in heaven there is no beer, that's why
we drink it here. I just hope this ain't gonna turn out like
fucking 'Nam where we come home and people fucking
boo us. Drop their heads in shame at our service. What's that
shit about? You want protection, you want your rights, your
freedom to say and do as you fucking please, but you think
you can get it sitting on your ass reading books? Reading
books by piss-ant left wing intellectuals who sooner run to
Canada than accept the responsibility and weight of their
beliefs. You think you can stop terrorism by blocking traffic?
Turning the other cheek? Circulating petitions? Is that how
you would have prevented the Holocaust? World War I? What
if the bad guys don't play by your rules? You probably voted

for Al Gore and you know what, if Al Gore was President, he'd still be thinking about it and thinking about it and thinking about it. Meanwhile, a terrorist with a bomb is in your house, sits on your bus, fires an AK-47 through your front window, kills your baby, then what? You want to think about it? You gonna offer him a fucking Diet Coke and say, hey, let's talk it out. Tell each other dirty jokes. Draw up a peace treaty. Bond. Fucking bullshit. Please, don't desecrate my uniform. Is there not a point in your life that you would fight? No, not me. I'm asking you. You personally. Think about it. What does it take to get you off your high and mighty ass and fight? Chew on that. Long and hard. In case I don't come back. Now, how about a beer? Anyone willing to buy me a beer? An American beer.

GOOD MOURNING, AMERICA
Lucy Wang

Dramatic
SCURVY, any age, Asian American

A few days after terrorists' attack on September 11, 2001, SCURVY is in line as he checks his travel destination options at an Amtrak train station.

SCURVY   My grandfather used to say there's no such thing as a bad orange in California. Of course, he used to say that as he tried to sell you a whole crate full of oranges. All kinds of oranges. Blood oranges. Valencias. Clementines. Satsumas. Navels. You can never have too much Vitamin C. You don't want to catch scurvy, do you? Scurvy. That was his favorite word. He used to cackle just saying it. Scurvy. Grandpa thought it was such a funny sounding word for something that means bleeding under the skin, bleeding gums. But scurvy ceased to be a barrel of laughs when the Japanese bombed Pearl Harbor. Suddenly my grandparents were considered high security risks and were taken away to internment camps. They lost their citrus orchard. They lost their sense of humor. So, when the second plane hit the World Trade Center, I grabbed my address book and pulled out a road map. I panicked. Where the hell am I going to go if the terrorists are Asian? Who will have the guts to protect me from illegal, immoral seizures? Do I know anyone with that kind of courage? I'm not sure I do, so I prayed to God. Please please, dear God, don't let the terrorists be Chinese, Japanese, Korean, Filipino, Vietnamese, Polynesian, anybody that remotely looks like me. Am I fucking ashamed that I jumped for joy when I learned the terrorists were Muslim? You betcha. Ideally, it shouldn't matter. Ideally, we're, above all, Americans. Ideally, it's innocent until proven guilty. Ideally, there are no bad oranges anywhere. Grandpa, you were definitely right about one thing, you can still die of scurvy. Scurvy also means worthless, mean, contemptible. Grandpa died at Manzanar, a victim of mean, worthless contempt.

GOOD MOURNING, AMERICA
Lucy Wang

Dramatic
KYLE, 21, male or female, any ethnicity

KYLE *has just turned 21. It's September 11, 2001.*

KYLE   Today was supposed to be my twenty-first birthday. I say supposed to because how could I possibly celebrate? I had been looking forward to this date for years. My friends planned to surprise me with a wild birthday bash—kegs of beer, strippers, fireworks. My wild party plans were blown to smithereens, my birthday fell apart with the collapse of hope and life. Turning twenty-one was supposed to be a defining moment. A day to remember. A day I'd get to look back and say, damn, those were the good ole days. My crazy carefree salad days. The days I danced atop bar tables, ran naked through water fountains, and clumsily swung for the stars. The days I embraced life with reckless abandon and lusty *joie de vivre*. Now I can't help but wonder, will I ever be allowed the privilege of enjoying my birthday again? Of being happy and silly on September 11? Or will the day I was born always be the day too many people died? I want to feel my age, an age of promise, of multiple choice. You can't reverse time, you only turn twenty-one once. But instead of feeling twenty-one, I feel fifty something. Like my life is half over. I've been robbed.

GOOD MOURNING, AMERICA
Lucy Wang

Dramatic
BETH, early 30s to mid-40s, any ethnicity

BETH *lost her kids in the Oklahoma City bombing. She is addressing* KENNETH FEINBERG, *lawyer in charge of the 9/11 Victim Compensation Fund, a week after September 11, 2001.*

BETH I love New York. New York is where I found myself. Where I fell in love. Dan and I used to see all the shows. Sip cappuccino in Little Italy, dim sum in Chinatown, Shakespeare in Central Park. New York was our adult Disneyland. We couldn't get enough of New York, of each other, so we tied the knot. Got married at the South Street Seaport with the Brooklyn Bridge lighting up the heavens. When we decided to have children, Dan and I thought maybe it was time to move somewhere where there'd be more space. More grass. More balance. Somewhere we could be normal. Safe. Somewhere we could afford day care. Dan was dropping Zack and Janey off at day care when an explosion ripped through the Alfred P. Murrah Federal Building, blowing them to smithereens. It was the worst terrorist attack on U.S. soil. April 19, 1995. 9:02 a.m. The blast could be felt over fifteen miles away. 168 victims killed. 500 people injured. Countless others lost friends and relatives. How was this loss memorialized? A wall with a reflecting pool. Small, empty chairs. Nine rows of chairs to represent the nine floors of the building. Chairs composed of bronze, stone, and glass. With the largest concentration of chairs in the center where the main impact of the bomb was greatest. The memorial is beautiful, sad, and now a stark reminder that Okies are worth much less than New Yorkers. Minimum a million dollars less. Where's my act of Congress? My trash bags filled with cold cash? Where's my check, Mr.

Feinberg? I lost three people, Mr. Feinberg. My entire family, my *raison d'être*. Why am I less worthy of sympathy and compensation? It's not about the money. It's about respect. It's about that gaping hole in my heart, the bottomless pit of loss. The rubble of grief that gives beneath your feet and threatens to swallow you whole. Don't turn away because you think I'm bitter and unconsolable. Turn away because you know as well as I do that no matter where you are, where you choose to live, raise a family, you are not safe and there's not a goddamned thing you can do about it.

GUILTY UNTIL PROVEN INNOCENT

Christine Toy Johnson

Dramatic

SAMANG CHENG ("SAM," for short), forty-three, Cambodian American

SAM's mother fled the Khmer Rouge in 1978 with SAM when he was five years old, leaving behind an older brother with her sister. A successful lawyer, he is ruled by a strong sense of justice while also combating survivor's guilt for having grown up with privilege in America. His Khmer name means "fortunate." SAM talks to his ex-wife ALICIA, an American social worker.

SAM   I can't stop thinking about how we would be treated now—if we were refugees now. What would have become of us? A young woman and her five-year-old son, running through minefields without a country to call their own. (*Beat.*) And then I wonder why, in the midst of having so much now . . . in the midst of that—how, why I can't ever seem to shake this, I don't know, this deep well of . . . it starts way down in the pit of my soul and circles around each one of my blood vessels till I can't breathe. So, I do more, work more, buy more. But nothing helps. "I need to be more grateful," I think. I'm healthy. I have all I could ever need. I'm alive, for God's sake. In America. (*Beat.*) When I came back here with you in 2008, I had the same impulse you did, to stay, to get to know my parents' country, to connect with whatever was here that I needed to connect to. But what I saw was . . .

(*He can't continue.*)

Three decades after Pol Pot, now almost four, the devastation, the decimation—it grabs you by the throat and it never lets you go. Remember the day we realized that no one we met over the age of thirty hadn't had their parents or brothers or sisters or teachers just . . . obliterated? Not one person. There's a new generation that's finally less directly in the line of fire, but it's like Vithu said to me the other day. "As if that fucking Pol Pot didn't leave his filthy footprints all over us." Back when I was here last time I thought, who am I? Am I Cambodian? Am I American? There's too much guilt associated with being either. So, I left and went back to someplace more comfortable, where I wouldn't have to think about it. Until now. I know I need to fight this case, Alicia. Not just for Vithu and Charya and you. And us. But for Arun. And my mother. Whatever it is that leaves us with this legacy of grief, for what our families have had to go through—whatever that is, it's all mixed up now with everything else I've learned about being a good American citizen—and it makes me feel like I have no other choice but to fight. But I don't know if I can, Alicia. I don't know if I can.

HALO HALLO BIRTHDAY
Christine Toy Johnson

Dramatic
ROWENA, 35, Filipina

ROWENA *is speaking as if she is present to her daughter,* GEMMA, *eight, who is back in the Philippines.*

ROWENA   I will send you everything, anything you need. I promised you that, remember? So always tell me what you need, you understand? Text me or write me or call me someday, will you? I wish you . . . I hope you will. I think you are worried about me and this is why you stopped writing to me. But don't worry, my sweet baby! I am okay. I think of you and your *Lola* and remember why I am here. I don't pay attention to how much I miss singing you to sleep, or the taste of your *Lola's* chicken adobo, or the smell of the top of your head! I don't pay attention to the smell of the cigarette smoke in the club, the smell of the liquor on their breath, the smell of all of them grabbing me and pulling at me and calling me . . .

(*She starts to break down.*)

If your *Tatay* could see me, he would die all over again.

(*Pulls herself together.*)

No. No. *Gina gawa ko dahil para sa familya ko.* He would know that I do this for you. I do this for him. For *Lola.* For all of us. But mostly for you. I'll tell you a secret, Gemma. Sometimes I talk to you like this and after, I feel like we've just spent a little time together! You, me, and Daddy. Like we'll be one day again, in heaven.

(*She hums a lullaby.*)

And I'll tell you another secret, baby. Sometimes I sing this song in my head when I am working. And I fill my head with pictures of you: my baby girl, running, playing, swimming . . . all the things I know you do without me. Without us. And you know what? It takes me right next to you, just for one minute. And I am happy. I am with you, and your Daddy and I are singing your favorite song to you, just like we did when you were born. The happiest day of my life. Do you know that this little song was the only thing that would stop your crying? It's true! Oh, how your Daddy could sing! So much better than me! And now, it stops my crying, too. (*Beat.*) I have to go now, baby. To work. So I can get that new uniform to you even sooner! And a special surprise I saw for you at the market yesterday! For your birthday! You'll see! (*Beat.*) I love you very much. *Mahal na mahal kita.* Happy Birthday, Baby.

THE HAUNTED WIDOW LINCOLN
Donna Latham

Dramatic
MARY TODD LINCOLN, 57

In her room in an asylum preparing tea, MARY TODD LINCOLN *speaks to ghosts of the past and present, including* QUEEN VICTORIA, PRESIDENT LINCOLN, *and her sons.*

MARY   Do you approve, Your Majesty? A woman of your breeding and stature appreciates decorous arrangement. Why, thank you, Your Highness. Your kind words touch my heart. Like you, I will honor my dead husband to my own dying breath. I've worn widow's weeds for ten years, and I'll wear them to the grave. I beg your pardon? (*Listens against wall.*) Oh, I daresay I agree. Most heartily. Dear Queen Victoria, you and you alone understand the depth of my despair. Only you know the imprints our loved ones have left on history. Today's parcel has arrived. Splendid, splendid. The apothecary in town is so kind. Camphor and laudanum, just as I requested. Excellent, just excellent! You've no idea how this pleases me, your Majesty. I would ask you to tea, but I realize it's not fitting and proper. Of course, this is a madhouse. Just how does one ascertain what is fitting and proper? Shall we read from *Hamlet* later, Ma'am? After I have tea with my family. I do enjoy the Dane's antic disposition. Yes, yes, we'll read together! Over a drop of sherry perhaps. That might aid my slumber. An Indian spirit yanks steel springs from my head and does not allow me to sleep. See the hole he's left? Tea time!

(*Arranges imaginary chairs around table, pulls out chairs, and seats "others" one by one.*)

Father, do be seated at the head of our table. You will ever be leader of our family and leader of our nation. Taddie, next to Father, please. No! Such a mischief-maker, darling boy. Mustn't touch the biscuits until they are served. Fold your hands in your lap. No wriggling like a tadpole. Ahem, Father! Elbows off the table. Remember? Frontier manners won't do in the city. Willie, Eddie, won't you join us? A little birdie told me there's sweet potato pie with fresh cream. Whose turn is it to say grace?

A HIT DOG WILL HOLLER
Inda Craig-Galván

Dramatic
GINA, late 30s to early 40s, African American

GINA *is speaking to* DRU*, a younger woman working as a delivery driver who's recently become* GINA*'s sole contact with the outside world.* GINA *suffers a "specific" form of agoraphobia and* DRU *asks her to explain what the roaring monster outside sounds like to her.*

GINA   You know how if you're standing outside and a fire truck passes? You hear it coming. Then it gets closer. Then it gets unbearable. Like your brain doesn't have room to hold any more siren sound. And then it gets right up on you. Even louder. Even less room inside but you feel like it's already taking up all of it. Every piece. But you're wrong. Because it just gets louder somehow. Like it's inside, inside your head driving its big, red, metal, loud parts straight through your mind. And then it's gone. And you think the pain in your ears and your head and your eyes and your nose—because it was everywhere—you think it's gonna linger. How could it not? But it doesn't. That's the messed-up part. It's like it never happened. You look up and everybody else is smiling and talking and walking along like it's nothing. Like it's nothing. It's nothing to them. And you're expected to just keep crossing the street or whatever you were doing. Just go on with your life. Business as usual. Like it never happened. Like it's not about to happen again at any moment. Like you won't open up the news to another one. And another. Every day for the rest of your life. And you know, or at least you think that it really is only a matter of days before it happens again. Then the days become always. And you're always afraid of the space in your brain being taken up. And torn apart.

A HIT DOG WILL HOLLER

Inda Craig-Galván

Dramatic
GINA, late 30s to early 40s, African American

GINA *explains to her editor,* CONSTANCE, *why she's not making the deadline for the book she's writing.* GINA*'s agoraphobia physically manifests as a roaring monster that we hear every time her front door is opened. By this point in the play, the young woman who's been delivering food to* GINA, DRU, *also experiences the same phenomenon that prevents her from continuing her role as an activist.*

GINA   Listen, Constance. I'm gonna be real with you. I need to take care of a friend. She's sick. And not just sick. She lost her way. She's lost everything. She can't go out. She can't make a difference and that's the one thing that she got into all of this for. I think. Hard to remember now, it's been so long since she's had to be real with herself. With anyone. And so, she forgot that. She forgot all about that in an effort to because she needed a roof and take-out and red bottoms. So, she forgot. It was easy to forget. And when she remembers . . . when she does remember the why and the what and the who then it all comes flooding back. Screaming back. Roaring. She realizes how far she's come or how far away she's gone or . . . she's gone. She's not her. She's not helping. She's not doing shit. She's not who she thought she'd be or who they thought she should be. She's tired. But she can't be tired. She's got strong African blood. Can't be tired. She's a woman. Can't be tired. She knows how to endure. It's in her motherfucking DNA. Can't be tired. If she is tired, then she's wrong. Somehow. It's her who's wrong. She's stuck on a couch. She won't get off of the damn couch. She won't go out. She's forgotten what the sky looks like. She's forgotten the clouds that look like sailboats. And now she hates herself. For being tired. And for being sick. Ridiculous, really. She hates herself for letting them win.

THE HOLDING SPACE
Kate Schwartz

Dramatic
MARFA, mid to late 50s

MARFA *is the wife of* BRONZE, *a deeply depressed man who makes coffins for a living. Today is the five-year anniversary of the untimely death of their child,* SARAH. BRONZE *never allowed his wife to grieve and often took out his pain and frustration on an innocent musician named* ROTHSCHILD. MARFA *cannot bear the sadness anymore, and prays to God for solace.*

MARFA   God, please listen to me. Can you help us? I'm worried sick about my husband. He's having these . . . these episodes. They're happening more frequently. Is he hallucinating? I can't seem to help him. He's angry, filled with rage. Five years, God. Five painful years. I can barely stand it anymore. I'm so lonely it hurts. It actually hurts physically. He used to be gentler, warmer. But, since that *day*, he's just so sad, God. He struck another man. He called him "Jewboy," then hit him. Bronze was taught to *hate* anyone who was different from him. When he tells me he's "proud of his heritage" it's just a guise for thinking his heritage is superior. Guide him, God. (*Pause.*) Or, can you guide him, my Sarah . . . our Sarah? *Why* does he ignore me? He's building his own coffin. Please . . . please . . . *please* . . . bring my Bronze back to life. I'm begging you, God. I'll do *anything*. (*Beat.*) Please, relieve Bronze and me from this debilitating grief and guilt regarding the death of our little girl. I'm finishing your portrait, Sarah. Wavy blonde hair, sweet gray eyes, lips shaped like a bow . . . Too loud . . . too much noise. Bronze. It's too loud. Bronze. Please stop. Too loud. My head hurts. (*Massages left arm.*) Something's not right . . . Bronze. Bronze. Come quickly.

HOUSE RULES
Cynthia Chapman

Dramatic
CARRIE, 20s

CARRIE *is best friends with* DAYENNE *from her high school days. She was a bad influence and ultimately her bad habits cost* CARRIE *her life.* CARRIE *lives on in* DAYENNE *as the projection of* DAYENNE's *gambling addiction.*

CARRIE   Do you hear that? That's the sound of a winner. The sound of euphoria, of sweet, sweet glory! What is your sound? Hmmm? It's the gnawing sound of defeat. It's the intolerable sound of whimpering, of a pitiful quitter. Is that what you want to feel? Don't you want the wins? Then don't be a quitter. You are not done until I say you are. Do you hear me? You need a bigger stake. Roulette was not your friend tonight. And no more incessant gibbering about your family. They despise you! But, look around. This is your family now. Got it? They don't judge you like everyone else. You see the ones? The ones masking their desperation behind vacant eyes? That's your family. There! And there. Look at that man. He's going through hell right now. A three-day bender. No sleep. He's lost everything and can't go home to his family because he's bankrupted them of their savings and dreams. You are from the same seed. You're all begging the machines to give you what you crave, to feel loved, because you can't get it from your family anymore. Now, get over to the slots and see what life is going to give you this time. The sound of glory is calling you.

I KNOW

Jacquelyn Reingold

Comic
DANIEL, 70s, but could be any age

DANIEL, *an actor, tells* LILA, *an actress with whom he lives, about an audition he had today.*

DANIEL   Hello Darling—happy to see you—I missed you— you look beautiful as always—no—*more* beautiful, though how that is even possible I cannot imagine. I had a helluvan actor's nightmare of a day, so to make things a little worse, I went shopping at Fairway. Remember when it was just a store with good produce, and all you had to fear were the crazy ladies with their carts? Now it has its own zip code, and every time I go, everything's been moved, so it makes even less sense than the no sense it used to make. You hungry? I thought I'd make a special "Daniel Raskin" dinner. With a back rub for dessert. You wouldn't believe the audition I had: some God-awful movie about Libyan terrorists living in an air pocket below the Hudson, who, when discovered by outer space aliens mate to create Mutant Terrorists poised to take over the world, and *I*, if cast, would have the memorable pleasure of playing a night watchman who utters the very important words "What are you doing here?" then gets killed by the Aliens' plutonium shooting third arm—for scale. So I went to my agent's office to suggest I not be submitted for such garbage, and, between phone calls, he told me that all the casting directors who say I'm a pain in the ass are wrong, which, of course, was his way of telling me what he really thinks of me, without actually saying it. He did, how- ever, mention five or six times, that if *you* were interested in changing your theatrical representation, since everyone loves *you,* he'd be thrilled to take you on and steal your ten percent. *So,* my dearest and amazing woman, here's to you, because above all else, no matter what happens, and how awful it is or might be, I adore you. As I enter the lobby, slip past our sleeping doorman, I'm filled with anticipatory delight, and when I step into the elevator, it's not the only thing that albeit, slowly, starts going up. How are you? What did you do today? Tell me everything. (*No answer.*) What's going on? Is it monologue night?

IDENTITY CRISIS
Royal Shirée

Dramatic
MAMA, late 40s

MAMA *grew up in the racist South. It wasn't until she met her husband,* VICTOR, *a very light-skinned black man, that she came to understand the power of love, faith, and wisdom, and understanding that hate can be all-consuming. Her daughter,* VICTORY, *has succumbed to self-hate, and she must put her power of faith to the test when sending* VICTORY *away to save her life. Here, she speaks of her personal journey of marrying* VICTOR *and raising their daughter without him.*

MAMA   Victory and her daddy downtown one day an' the wind just blowed off her hat to the street. Her daddy run to grab her when a car knocked him down. The hospital folk kept askin' for his wife and I told 'em I's here. Here Um is. My baby girl justa screamin' and cryin'. There was no comfortin' her. Heard her call me mama and seent her head on my breast. I seent the shame in my baby's eyes for me. My husband bled to death. My baby girl hurt to death. Seems I lost two souls in one day. Never been the same. Life's been hard, but it sho has been good. All these years done pass and all colored folk and all white folk ain't been blessed with eyes God give me and my Victor. Seems we been fightin' all our lives, don't make much sense to be fightin' each other. Ya see, devil come in colors, too. I may be old, but some thoughts ain't new. Don't see my baby much no mo'. Too young to know the world, too black to know herself. I been hearin' the sweet songs of angels now, too weak to worry. I asked God to get in front of my baby and told Satan to get thee behind 'cause Victory is mine.

IDENTITY CRISIS
Royal Shirée

Dramatic
MAMA, late 40s

MAMA *grew up in the racist South. It wasn't until she met her husband,* VICTOR, *a very light-skinned black man, did she come to understand the power of love, faith, and wisdom, and understanding that hate can be all-consuming. Her daughter,* VICTORY, *has succumbed to self-hate, and she must put her power of faith when sending* VICTORY *away to save her life. Here, she speaks of her personal journey of marrying Victor and raising their daughter without him.*

MAMA   I know this because the blood I saw were the tears of my grandbabies that would never see how cold and cruel this world could be, or how beautiful and precious life should be. I saw my own innocence die with my babies and my grandbabies because I wanted to be with people that I could never or would ever want to be like. That was the day a part of me died and the day I began to hate me and my name. And it's funny, because it was also the day that I was born. Well, Judas and his friends just took me home and threw me out in front of the house without even stoppin' the car. I can still hear them laughin' and singin'". . . Victory is Mine, Victory is Mine . . ." Mama ran out of the house and got me from the front yard, cleaned me up and called her sister up here in New York who said we can come. I remember the pain in Mama's eyes that she bore from my pain. I remember her rubbing my hair and rockin' me sayin', (*In Mama's voice.*) "Honey-chile. It's gonna be all right now. Can't nuthin' hurt you again because I'm takin' your pain away from here and leavin' you with everythin' I know." I was too tired to try to figure out what she meant this time. The next day, she told me that her sister was expecting me within the next day or so, but that she was too tired to make the trip. She told me not to be scared because God and Mama would always be with me. What I learned on the long bus ride was that I felt Mama when I left, or maybe it was when she left, and I felt God when He came. Then it was as if she told me right then and there, or maybe I realized right then and there, that I got it. I understand. I won. I am the victor and Victory is good. I know now that I don't have to change who I am, but just be who I am.

(*Embracing herself.*)

". . . Victory is mine. Victory is mine. Victory is mine."

JANE

Annie LaRussa

Dramatic
JANE, 19–22

JANE *was raped at a frat party.* JOE, *her boyfriend, helped* JANE *after the attack and gave her a blanket to wrap herself in.* JANE *is returning the blanket to Joe at his dorm.* JOE *is trying to convince her to go to the police.*

JANE I went to the door of the police station. I never went *in* the police station. I remembered Zoey had nightmares after she was . . . Zoey had these nightmares that people were throwing rocks at her, that she was being stoned to death. I told her that no one does that anymore. Don't be ridiculous, Zoey. Go to the police. I kept telling her that. Go to the police, go to the police, go to . . . I understand now. I feel sick and sad for her. I also strangely feel guilty that now she'll feel bad for me. She'll feel like it was her fault. And it's not her fault. It's not my fault. Right? Right? I go from acceptance to denial so quickly that I'm exhausted . . . and confused. I'm trying . . . Do what's RIGHT . . . I keep saying over and over. It's not my fault . . . But deep down . . . I feel stupid, and out of control, and needing to be punished, because of my "behavior," my short, short skirt, my ME who brought this all on! . . . I am so disgusting . . . I don't want this body anymore . . . I don't know this body . . . this piece of flesh . . . this . . . this . . . hole . . . that he found and took advantage of . . . this . . . hole that he filled with . . . I don't want this body anymore.

LOOKING FOR THE PONY

Andrea Lepcio

Dramatic
LAUREN, 40

LAUREN *has been battling breast cancer for three years and fears she is coming close to dying. She is talking to her sister who she trusts will take care of her family as best she can.*

LAUREN   No high school ball, for Noah, no major league career. What will it be? What will he find? High school, he's hit his stride, asks me to check his work less, he has more confidence, more perspective, he gets anxious like you, you'll help him. Things he wants to accomplish, he's so well rounded. Noah's okay. I talked to Eli's teachers. They all had Noah—such a different mechanism. Eli feels his way through the world. He wants the Big Boy furniture for his books, he reads so fast, and his designs . . . He's young, he's himself, he'll . . . my. Those nineteen years sure flew. Flew. We made. Those boys. All those boys. We made and made and made. I'm going to get him that barbecue he's been eyeing. Probably be too busy to use it, but he'll have it. Some substitute. All those first days. So many first days ahead. You'll take them shopping. When Joe's busy. If they need . . . You'll take them. I . . . would like to go to the Westminster Dog Show. I'd like to get my M.B.A. I want to read your literary magazine. I want to be mother of the groom. I want to get kissed again in the Jardin du Luxembourg.

MARILYN MONROE IN THE DESERT
Barbara Blatner

Comic
MARILYN, 30s

*An Everywoman MARILYN MONROE, finding herself in a surreal
desert, thinks she's making a movie and improvises for the cameras.*

MARILYN Uh, the wind is hot, dry—ferocious! And the American desert is savage! And it never ends, and stretches further than the eye can see! And its heat never bends! Except in mirages, oo! I love mirages! And I love heat, the right kind of heat, heat without end, amen! And Hollywood was, um, born in the desert, with the cowboy and Indian movie! And Hollywood gives me horses a-runnin' and guns a-shootin', and lone beautiful men, ah men! And the cowboy will eternally click his hot spurs across the silver screen, and the Indian find water in the dust! And like the cowboy and Indian, the onscreen, r-e-e-l Marilyn will be eternal as you see her now! Young, gorgeous and never old! No crow's feet or cellulite for MM, just celluloid into infinity, oo! And young beautiful Marilyn will forever seek her one true love who will . . . uh . . . um . . . help her love herself at last. But wait: Didn't the real Indian get . . . um . . . thrown out of the desert, and aren't real-life cowboys kinda finished these days? And won't the real desert, 'cause we're wrecking it, dry up and life there be kaput?! So, what is eternal? What about the r-e-a-l Marilyn?! She's not gonna get old and die a disgusting natural death, is she?! Oh no you can't let her fade like the Indian and cowboy and desert, Mr. Director! Promise you'll shoot her—boom! With a gun, not a camera. If one dimple shows on her derrière, right? If you don't, she'll just kill herself before she gets old. If she's old and ugly, no one will want her and she'll never find the one true love who will heal her soul.

MARRYING KIND
Andrea Lepcio

Dramatic
BUCK, 34

BUCK *has loved and lost* LILY *a number of times. He finally knows what he wants.*

BUCK   This obsession. I think by now we can call it an obsession of mine. My girlfriends. We'd talk about kids. I'd say how many do you want and they'd be like two or three. And I was always like okay, I'll get them up to four or five. Twins do run in my family. I fantasized. Constantly. Drove them away. Likely. And I get your journey and what you've been through. How it's been for you? Men, I think, we have no idea what women really go through. Was I? Did I somehow hurt my girlfriends in some way I didn't understand? I hate that mars venus crap. I want to think we can understand each other. Maybe there's stuff I miss. I'm just. This has been my. Whole reason. For forever. With. Out. Thought. I guess. It was what I wanted. Children. Boatloads of children. All I pictured. When I looked out and saw my life. That was it. A job. A way to make a decent living to feed everyone. But it was always for everyone. For the lot of them. My lot. No other image. No other idea. From childhood. From birth. Whatever. That was it. No debate, no consideration, no question, no nothing. Till. Now. Now. Since I met you. I could tell. I could tell. What you said. Different things you said. I could tell. I could feel. With you. I just wanted. You. I didn't want the babies. Not that I didn't want the babies. But. For the first time. In my life. It was. You. Were. Enough. You were. The answer. You were what I wanted. Full stop. You.

MARRYING KIND
Andrea Lepcio

Dramatic
LILY, late 20s

LILY *is speaking to* BUCK, *who has been unhappily married to*
DAWN *and* LILY *has been unhappily in love with him. Suddenly
tonight, he has broken free and come to her.*

LILY   I'm a scaredy-cat. I am. I know I'm a lobsterman. I know I
graduated college. But everything. Lots of things. Scare me.
And maybe everyone is just as scared as I am. That. Kind
of doesn't matter. Because I'm scared. Almost too scared
to. Choose. And I know I have made some classically bad
decisions. I should never have married Rod. I should never
have slept with Rod. But if I hadn't, I wouldn't have had the
experience of being pregnant. Of expecting. Of suddenly
wanting. My child. Unless some other guy got me pregnant.
I do seem to be fertile. I should never have smiled at the guy
who raped me. Before. I smiled before. It wasn't an invita-
tion, but he didn't know that or didn't care. Regrets, I guess.
I regret the decisions I've made and I'm petrified of the
decisions I have to make. And I almost ran away. I came so
close. You stopped me. But I came so close. Like that would
make everything better to leave. Even though leaving was
the last thing I wanted to do. So somehow, I listened when
you asked me not to. Gin told me I could be happy. That I deserved to be happy. What does that even? Deserve. Not how
my family operated. Happiness. Is just not a particular habit
of mine. A usual thing. A goal, even. If I'm out on the sea. I'm
fine. Isn't being fine, fine? I used to think it was. Until. You've
kind of ruined my life in six ways. First, I'm in love with you
and I've never had that feeling of falling like this. Don't. Say.
Any. Thing. Second, I'm thinking I could live with you and I'm

very messy and I can see from your truck and how you made dinner that you're uber neat, so there's that. Could I learn? I don't know. Could you learn? I don't know. Third, you make me think of babies. Fourth, you make me scared I'll miscarry again and have that no funeral loss pain again. Fifth, you make me believe I can make a baby and love a baby with you and raise a baby and know the person this baby will become for the rest of my life. Sixth, I'm scared I can't give you as many babies as you want and I'm scared with you I'll want more babies than I ever wanted and we'd still be having babies during climate change so we have to fight that to make life better for our babies.

MERMEN
T. Cat Ford

Dramatic
LYNWOOD MURPHY, 70s

LYNWOOD, *owner of a Florida alligator farm and a self-styled preacher, begs his girlfriend* VANESSA *to take him back.*

LYNWOOD   Vee? Vee? I had to see you. I had to 'cause . . . I spent all last night wrangling gators. My farm was flooded. It was a sight. Gators floated over the top of their pens and out, out . . . by the time I got there they were floating around in the gift shop. The smarter ones on the roof. Gators . . . everywhere, on the benches of the pavilion . . . in the parking lot. They didn't know what to do with themselves and neither did we. They're sorted by size for their pens. How the hell were we going to do that!?! This wasn't Noah's ark. They were not going to go two by two. Then a miracle, nothing less than a miracle was visited on us. I heard a gator hiss. Then another. We ran toward the pens and there they were— trying to get back in! They were banging on the wire mesh, bloodying their noses. They wanted to go home! I've never seen anything like it. They thought that pen was home. They didn't know it was a prison. All these years they never tried to get out, but nothing, I promise you, nothing was going to keep them from getting back in! It took us hours, hours . . . we worked all night. Desperate animals, blood. They're home now. Even a dumb alligator has an idea of home. It may be just a prison, but to them it's . . . I watched them and it broke what was left of my heart. Because now I . . . I learned from those dumb animals. I learned. God visited a lesson on me. My home is with you Vee and I got to make you see that. At this stage of my life, I don't have to accept something that I know is dead wrong and I just ain't going to do it 'cause we live in the Age of Grace not the Age of Law. Do you know what that means? It means that in olden times the Bible said we had to follow rules and laws covering everything. There were certain things we were not supposed to eat; animals with cloven hoofs—pigs, lobsters, shrimps and so on. But then God Almighty in His wisdom sent us our savior and He brought with him the Age of Grace and now we can eat shrimps, Maine lobsters if we can get them, we can even eat crawdads! Jesus did that for us. He made this the Age of Grace. God's grace! God's love rules us now and that's the only rule we have to live by! Jesus washed us in his glorious blood and if you can't see I'm washed, you are as wrong as those Israelites wandering in the desert. 'Cause you and me together is a gift from God and it's a sin not to accept a gift from God. A grave sin! I love you, woman. And I won't let you sin! I am not going to stand idly by while you refuse God's glorious grace! "God said it was not good for man to be alone. And the Lord God caused a deep sleep to fall upon Adam, and he slept; and he took one of his ribs, and closed up the flesh instead thereof. And the rib, which the Lord God had taken from man, made her a woman, and brought her unto the man. And Adam said, 'This is now bone of my bones, and flesh of my flesh: she shall be called Woman, because she was taken out of Man.' And they were both naked, the man and his wife, they were one flesh and they were not ashamed." Oh no, my Lord. No! I'm not ashamed. I love you, woman! Do you hear me? I love you!! And it may be a prison but I am coming home!

THE NEW DEAL
Christine Toy Johnson

DRAMATIC
ABIGAIL LEE, mid-20s, Chinese American

ABIGAIL *talks to her late grandfather whom she addresses as "Goon Goon" (pronounced "Goong Goong" in Cantonese), whose spirit has appeared to her in a moment of crisis.*

ABIGAIL   I mean, in this moment, I can see that standing in front of a bulldozer isn't maybe as poetic as it sounded the moment before I did it. But it beats not *wanting* to do it, right? This is the whole point of you showing up right now, isn't it? To tell me whether or not I should literally stand up for . . . where I've come from? All this time, whenever someone's said, "But where are you really from?" I've said, "Brooklyn. New York. The United States of America." But the real answer is: *You*, isn't it, Goon Goon? I come from You. And the footprints you left for us to walk in, made out of the sheer will to make something out of nothing. I never knew what you meant when you used to say "She who knows where she comes from, knows where she comes from." But is that it? Is that what you wanted me to remember? Because I just don't know if I have the . . . if I can live up to that. (*Softly.*) Can you forgive me if I can't?

OFF THE MAP
Christine Foster

Dramatic
ANGELA, early 20s

ANGELA *is a grad student in archaeology, on a field survey in Central America. She is talking to* CLAIRE*, an unhappy retiree who is living with her husband in the jungle.*

ANGELA   It's bad luck to try to save money. My sister . . . we went to the movies one Saturday . . . when I was eleven and she was thirteen . . . and she was pretending to be twelve, to get in for the kid rate, she was almost the same size as me. Very skinny. So, the ticket lady asked her how old she was and she said, "twelve . . . how old are you?" We thought that was sooo funny. We laughed so hard we had to run to the washroom. Anyway, she got in for four-fifty. So, we saved. We saved big. Two whole bucks. Three days later she was dead. Meningitis. They think she caught it there, at the movies. I mean, how? It wasn't that crowded. I didn't get it. We weren't supposed to be there, either. My parents didn't like us going to the movies. They were very religious. But we were dying to see it—an outdoor adventure . . . with cougars and grizzly bears. We lived in the city but Amy loved the outdoors . . . Nature. She would have loved it here. The monkeys, the hummingbirds. She had pictures of animals all over her room. Not rock stars or actors, but birds of prey . . . alligators, even. And she was so good at school, too, much smarter than me. And you should have seen her play softball. She could do anything, really. She was an eagle among sparrows. She should be here. You have your husband and your daughter, and everyone's still breathing—and you feel empty?

ON THE ROAD TO HOLENESS
J. Lois Diamond

Dramatic
DIANE, 28

DIANE *is a shiatsu massage therapist. She has just broken up with her boyfriend* JEFF *and is speaking to her friend* SWAMPSCOTT BETTY, *a rigid New Age fanatic.*

DIANE   God, I don't even know what to think anymore. Sometimes, I feel like I have this hole, kind of a vacuum, this overwhelming emptiness I can't fill, and I mean, if the man you're supposedly sharing your life with follows none of the values you're struggling to adopt, you just start to feel . . . disengaged, kind of like being in exile, like there's no place for you, sort of like Solzhenitsyn. I mean, the holistic types are sometimes a little fanatical . . . but he can be so all-American suburban fast food carnivore mainstream, and well, I certainly can't relate to that, and I wonder why I'm with him, why he's more attractive to me than, let's say, a healer. It's strange. He has a darker side, and sometimes, I think it's the most important thing we share. There's something about being with him. I'm frightened of that hole, and sometimes when we're together, it starts to fill up. Of course, that never lasts, and I'm left with it again. Sometimes, I have healing moments, and the hole closes for a little while. The feeling never lasts, but sometimes, for a moment, you get this bolt that says, there is logic to this universe. Life seems to have meaning and purpose. You know what I mean?

OPTIONS
Carol S. Lashof

Seriocomic
ELLEN, 18

ELLEN, *a high achieving high school senior, fears that college will
entail even more stress than she's dealing with now. So, in conversation with a classmate, she's reviewing her options.*

ELLEN I'm thinking maybe I'll go with having a prom baby.
You know, a baby conceived on prom night. On purpose,
or not on purpose, or sort of accidentally on purpose. Think
about it. Almost eight months of vacation. Everybody else
would be pulling all-nighters in college, and I'd be sitting on
the couch eating bon bons and watching TV, waiting for my
cute little baby to come. No problem sets on electricity and
magnetism. No research papers on the effects of genetically
modified food on the economies of Southeast Asia. No 5:00
a.m. crew practice. So what if babies cry and spit up and
poop all over everything and need to be fed in the middle
of the night? How bad can that be, sitting in a rocking chair,
humming a lullaby, compared to freezing your buns off in
the middle of a lagoon and rowing 'til your arms fall off. Anyway, most babies sleep through the night after a few weeks,
right? Or a few months at least. College is four years of not
getting enough sleep, followed by—what? Med school? Law
school? Grad school? Followed by—what? Marriage, kids,
career . . . Why not get the baby part out of the way sooner
rather than later? While you can still live with your parents,
and they can buy the groceries. I haven't talked to Daniel
about it. I figured I'd just sort of forget to bring the condoms
. . . He won't bring them. Daniel? Get real!

O.T.D. (OFF THE DERECH)
Shari Albert

Dramatic
LOLA, 40s

LOLA LIPSHITZ *is in her 40s. She's a children's book author who hasn't written a word in a couple of years. Her mother is dying of cancer and she hasn't visited her in the hospital because she can't deal with death after losing her beloved Lhasa Apso nine months ago. This is the opening of the play and she is addressing the audience.*

LOLA   I don't want to alarm anyone, but I smell gas. Does anyone else smell it? Don't light a cigarette or this whole place will be engulfed in flames in no time! I am Lola Lipshitz and I am terrified of fire. I think it would be the most horrendous way to go—burning alive. You'd smell yourself dying. I can't think of anything more frightening than that . . . Except maybe throwing yourself out a window. I always wonder if people change their minds on the way down. I don't want to die; I just don't want to live anymore. These are not the same thing. Death is so . . . permanent. Not wanting to live still has a glimmer of hope, the promise of if you hang on long enough, there might be a fabulous eleventh-hour musical number with hats and feathers and if you killed yourself before that happened, you'd feel quite cheated. I often think about it . . . not wanting to live. My dog died nine months ago and I still cry daily. It's hard to leave the apartment because the slightest suggestion of anything dog-like in my periphery sends me into convulsions of tears so I wear very dark sunglasses when I have to go outside. I am a forty-four-year old woman with no husband or children and my longest relationship was with my sixteen-year-old Lhasa Apso. And please don't say, "Go get another dog. There are so many who need homes." I KNOW THAT! DO I LOOK

LIKE A FUCKING IDIOT?! Sorry. I've been quick to anger lately. I didn't mean to yell . . . My mother has cancer. Stage four pancreatic, there's nothing that can be done. She doesn't have long to live and I hate her. She's a raging narcissist and I knew that from a very early age. When I was little, she'd take me shopping. I'd hide in racks of clothes, trying to get lost. I'd wait until after my mother screamed bloody murder for me to show myself, then I'd pop out of the racks of blouses and sensible slacks. I'd pretend to be deaf.

(*Speaking like a deaf person.*)

"Mama, you know I can't hear you!" Then she'd stomp on my foot really hard in her high heels and people would see her for the monster she was. I know I should visit her in the hospital but with the dog dying, it's just all too much . . . death. I do need to get out of here though. There is a dank stench of despair with a hint of hopelessness lingering in the air. Don't you smell it? Where does one go when one needs to be around people to know they're not actually dead . . . just to feel a little alive?

OTHER THAN WE

Karen Malpede

Dramatic
TANAKA, 20s–30s

In the future, a few years after the Deluge, a full-scale climate disaster, in a hermetically sealed, highly surveilled and strictly controlled Dome which the characters manage to escape in order to birth and raise their newbies in a fragile new clearing, TANAKA, a refugee, formerly a physician, from far away (Africa, Asia), has been allowed in to do menial labor and so that the radiation concentration in his bones can be monitored and studied. He has also engineered a way for men to nurse infants. This speech takes place after his nursing scene, an experience of intimacy that allows him to confront his past.

TANAKA　I saw my family swept away in the Deluge, after the rains, in the winds, the floods, the water rushed. A little girl of three with the brightest, roundest, blackest eyes in the world. I was holding her hand. My wife, a woman of such intelligence and instinct, we often needed barely to speak. We read one another's minds. With our son in her arms, a fat, smiling baby, fed at the same breasts where I had often suckled myself. They were gone while I watched it, was I trying to swim, was I . . . I do not know . . . I saw the water like a wall, a force I had never seen before . . . I must have let go. Many have seen what I did. Did what I . . . Many have lost everything. Most. Let go. But there is worse. On the road, walking inland, walking uphill, staggering away from the sea, a woman, battered by branches, cut and scarred, seaweed stuck in her hair, asked if I might carry her child. She had a baby in her arms and she felt she could not go on. She wished to pass the child to me. Maybe I could carry it somewhere. I was walking. I was strong enough. I passed her. I acted as if I had not heard. Perhaps, she had not said anything at all.

Perhaps, she had only looked and I saw as I used to see with my wife without words what was needed. I walked faster, as fast as I could walk, I walked away from her. I believe she sat down with her child to die as I walked past. (*Silence.*) *Homo sapiens* became narrow-minded and selfish. They grew to think only of their own selves. They became limited in their compassion. I wished to go on, mechanically walking, without wanting, I walked, I kept on walking. Saving myself. We cannot think ahead; we cannot stop ourselves from grasping. We are afraid of death; we walk away, we walk past the suffering of those not us. The suffering of others does not touch us as long as we walk. We refuse to look. Even without a future, even without a plan, I walked on and on. One day it came to me, something slight, I began for the first time in a long time to be able to hear my heart beat. I began to walk in tune with that. I thought, suddenly, it was not thought, it was feeling welling up, and I knew there will come a day, a time to come, when this ignorance will end, when the heart and the head will beat inside in unison, a thrum, thrum. It might not happen to us. I had given up on people, on myself, I had given up. But I understood, there will come a different moment, a turning, in years, perhaps sooner than we dare to wish, when life reasserts itself, and there will come a new, a noble race, of creatures who are capable of living fully, who want the best for others, who understand themselves as a part of, not apart from, who neither fear nor despise, who recognize, who bear their lives gladly, willingly, with restraint, and with joy welling up and they will be happy and fearless, careful, generous and kind.

PARADISE

Laura Maria Censabella

Dramatic
YASMEEN, 17, Muslim

YASMEEN *is addressing* DR. ROYSTON, *her biology teacher.*

YASMEEN   I never thought I could even *like* science. The first
day of your class I . . . I didn't know what you were talking
about. I didn't even know what a cell was! I just . . . I just
remember sitting at the end of class and thinking, Yasmeen,
you're gonna fail this, for the first time in your life you're gonna fail a class, and I was almost like . . . I was paralyzed. And
on the way home I said to myself I can either turn it around
and not be afraid of this, treat it exactly how I taught myself
every other thing, or I . . . So I stopped at the library and
took out every single book I could get my hands on and that
night I sat for like six hours after everyone in my family went
to sleep. I started with *Biology for Dummies* and that . . .
that gave me the confidence, and I remember just moving
up and up and up from bacteria to . . . to cells to complex
organisms and I was opening up to a whole new world. I
couldn't stop reading science books, and every night after
that. And in your labs, I couldn't get over it, looking at this
hidden world of the structure of things, and all of a sudden, I
had this hatred in me because I wasn't exposed to this for so
. . . for all these years . . . we almost never in grammar school
. . . I felt like I had missed out on it, like it was taken away
from me and I became obsessed and ever since that point,
I almost feel like I went over the edge with it. And I thought
you could tell . . . I thought you could see that I *got* what
you're talking about. Every class after that, it was like *you* just
talking to *me*. And then when you didn't know me, I thought
that . . . that must've been all in my head and I was nuts for

imagining that you . . . were so *wise*. But then I read your book. And I saw that you were funny, and way smarter than anybody I've ever met and . . . and maybe a little sad. But I'm a little sad too so I . . . so I get that. (*Pause.*) And I figured out the kind of science I want to do. Because of you. I wanna . . . I wanna look at the brain—the structures—to help people. Not like with diseases but with like how to live. Like you do. With like how to live.

POOLSIDE
T. Cat Ford

Comic
BRENDA, 30s

BRENDA *shares her worst fears with her best friend* ANN *as they watch their children play in the golf club pool.*

BRENDA   (*Off.*) Justin, behave! (*To another mother.*) Did you hear about Laura Dean? She ran over Mr. Thompson. (*Off.*) Justin get out of the pool right now if you are going to act that way! (*To the other mother.*) Why do little boys find their weenies so interesting? Oh well . . . Friday night, Mr. Thompson was trying to cross Patterson Avenue and Laura Dean hit him with her new Jag. Can you believe it? I can't wait until Justin starts doing things like that to embarrass me. I mean, think about it. Today he's in the golf club pool pulling down his bathin' suit every chance he gets, and he's only eight. No telling what he'll do in a few years. You know, I told Maureen not to get a sixteen-year-old child a Jag, but she just wouldn't listen to me. I believe they had to put Mr. Thompson in the hospital in Valdosta, him being so old and all. Laura hit him good. Maureen is just beside herself and she should be! I don't know what I'd do. I certainly wouldn't be able to go downtown to shop. There is one good thing about this entire episode. Mr. Thompson only made a tiny dent. Isn't that nice? He was always so considerate. I do hope he survives. I'd just hate for Maureen and Laura Dean to have to move to Atlanta and live with all those Yankees. (*Off.*) I see you Justin. That's real good honey-pie. (*To the other mother.*) Honestly, sometimes I worry about his brain.

THE QUADROON AND THE DOVE
Charlene A. Donaghy

Dramatic
CLARICE, 31, light-skinned African American

CLARICE *is speaking with* SAGE-FEMME, *the wise sentient who helped raise her. Failing to gain* SAGE-FEMME's *sympathy for her adversities, nor approval of her planned deceptions,* CLARICE *vows to make her own destiny.*

CLARICE Destiny? I've been hearing that from you all my life. But there must be a way to change what is already written. I have to believe that even if no one else does. My mama believed in *plaçage** because that's all she knew so of course I would follow the same path. But I got lucky. I fell in love with my patron. And I found another who would ease the pain when he went to his wife. Are we ever meant to care for just one person? I try to comfort so many. Lucien. Charlie-smith. Dove. Ellie. You. But with all my education and travel and trying to please everyone, the things you all seem to want are the things I cannot give you. How do I release Charlie-smith and Ellie when our lies can cost me my life? How do I allow Juliette to be a *placée** when I know that choice will bind her in ways that will take away both of our freedoms? She might rise but I will surely fall like mama when her patron died. We were almost destitute until Lucien took me, so I know, firsthand, what it is like to be put out. I vowed never to be that deserted. How do I make you, who can read the leaves and predict whatever you think our destiny might be, see that I must do what is best for me? Juliette cannot have my life. And I will take my secrets to my grave. I will never give up on what I want and if that means changing what you think is already written, so be it.

*Plaçage was a social practice of interracial unions in New Orleans and other French and Spanish colonies in the Caribbean. *Placée* was the term for women in these arrangements.

ROAR LIONS! ROAR!
T. Cat Ford

Dramatic
JONES, 19–20

JONES, a football player at a Southern University, begs his speech teacher to let him retake a test he failed.

JONES I'm just here 'cause I need to retake my test. I mean, you know, my test? See . . . I guess knowing the bones of the, I mean the cartilage of the throat box, uh, the voice box, the, the larynx, I guess that's a good thing, but I can't really see what knowing that is going to do to help me make a living. I'm working now and I ain't supposed to be. Coach don't know. Nobody knows. I'm getting chased by dogs all over this damn—'scuse me—darn town doing a survey for the City Directory. Going into people's fancy houses. People's shacks. One woman, she was so poor she didn't have 'lectricity or running water. Had a big fire going in the middle of the room to cook her something to eat and it ninety degrees. Sweat running down her face and on down her . . . Would knowing the bones of the throat box help her? I don't think so. I don't think so at all. And I'm asking her how many people live in that shack for the City Directory, and she says herself and points to what I thought was a little pile of dirty rags in the corner, which I see ain't rags. It ain't rags at'all. It's squawking and sweating too. And I say two. O.K. Two. And I ask if they got a phone number. Shit! I mean shoot, they don't even got 'lectricity. I got chased by two big-assed dogs that day and didn't even mind. I'm getting me an education. Yes siree! Yesterday I'm in a fancy neighborhood and this woman asks me in to answer my questions. I'm trying to be polite so I go in and I can't get out! There she is all dressed up in her fancy house, serving me cake, cookies, and co'cola and showing me the pictures of her grandchildren. She's all alone and talking to beat the band about her children, her grandchildren. Which obviously don't give a warm sh-shoot about her or she'd be talking to them. She could talk good too. She might have even known the names of her throat bones, but, hell/heck, I'll tell you this right now, it don't do her one damn/dang bit of good if all she's got to talk to is me, 'cause I hate the sound of her fucking—her voice! So what I'm trying to say is, I'll learn this bone shit/stuff. I'll learn all I got to. I don't know why I got to, but I will. I'll learn it. That's the point isn't it? Just to fuck—uh, uh, uh learn it?

SAM

Victoria Z. Daly

Dramatic
SAM, late 30s

SAM, *a surgeon just returned from World War II, has surprised his wife MIMI by showing up at their house unannounced, after several years away during the war. She's been avoiding him, and he wants to get her upstairs into bed.*

SAM   Mimi, I dreamed about you. In my bed. On my walks. Even in surgery, sometimes. Don't get me wrong, no one ever died, not because I dreamed of you. But sometimes when I sewed up a leg, or a soldier with his ear blown off, even though I was awake I dreamed I was touching your skin, breathing in your hair, hearing your heart beat. It was like I'd sew up a chest here, and a head there, and repair an artery, or sew fingers back on, and all these parts, if I put them together, somehow they'd add up to . . . I just needed . . . I needed . . . They were men. They weren't you. But if I kept sewing, and repairing, at some point, I'd have . . . I don't know . . . something. And that guy—with the sewn-on scalp and the sewn-on leg, and the missing eye, and the bullets in the chest, he's been lying next to me at night all the way on the boat from Algiers to England to New York and sitting with me on the train here . . . Let's go upstairs. I'll rest with you. Let's go upstairs, together. Now.

SAM
Victoria Z. Daly

Dramatic
SAM, late 30s

SAM, *a surgeon just returned from World War II, is on a blind date with GRACE, who comes from a wealthy family. He's trying to convince her that he's her destiny.*

SAM   You want to stay safe? Me—I keep you safe. You know the basic premise of medicine? Not healing. It's loss. If in any given case I think of everything that can go wrong, in the long run one of them will. Kill you off. No one wants to think about that, so I do it for you. It's like . . . like I'm in a giant game of baseball. Bottom of the ninth, bases loaded, two outs, and I'm at bat. Count of three and two. If I strike out, game's over. Season's over. The ball hurtles at me, ninety miles an hour. Might brush me back, might hit me in the head. If I swing and get lucky, I could knock it out of the park. But honestly, what do I do? Foul it off. Keep my eye on the ball, foul it off. Over and over. Keep the game going. Every day, I see disease, death—the worst things imaginable— coming towards you, and I stop it. It's not glamorous, but it's heroic. That's America. That's freedom. I keep you safe.

SCRAPBOOK JUNKIES
Elizabeth Dement

Seriocomic
DORIS, 30s–40s

DORIS *addresses a general membership meeting of the Parent Teacher Association.*

DORIS Good evening. I'm Doris Kahan—but I guess most of you know that already. I'm sorry. Well, anyway, I'm here, as Bonnie said, to give the treasurer's report for Bob, who isn't here. Thank you, by the way, Bonnie for that lovely introduction. It's nice to be a part of the PTA. Very grounding. Um, I should tell you, though, that Bob is not out of town, like Bonnie said. He's in town. I saw him this morning. When he gave me the figures here . . .

(*She holds up a piece of paper.*)

   . . . to give to you. So anyway . . . (*Pause.*) So, Bob didn't leave town, he's here, he just needed to take some time off. He's with his wife, Janet. I think a lot of you have met Janet, she's very striking. And tall. Anyway, Janet and he are having some . . . thing of a time. And well, I'm still here and he's with her, so I'll just give you the figures he gave to me to give to you. I'm sorry. I don't know why I felt compelled to tell you that. It just seemed like the situation was not accurate, or at least the description of the situation. There was more to it than just that he was out of town. "Oh, Bob's out of town, again, ha-ha, Doris will give the treasurer's report. Good old Doris." Anyway, so while Bob is with his wife doing God knows what, I will tell you that . . .

(*She looks at the papers.*)

   . . . the bagel sale brought in a whopping $73.25, which is half as much as our bake sale made last semester. I was in charge of the bake sale. It was Bob's idea to have a bagel sale this semester. But, unfortunately, it didn't do as well. I couldn't say why, really. I mean, there aren't a lot of Jews in this school. Bob isn't even Jewish . . . but of course, his wife is, so maybe that had something to do with it. Anyway, I guess that it's not so bad to lose a little money in the interest of cultural diversity. Maybe next time we can have an egg roll sale. Sandy—you're half Japanese, right? You could be in charge of that. Anyway, as I was saying, we made $73.25 from Bob's stupid bagel sale. But we have the spring picnic coming up, which always brings in a lot of money from hot dog sales. Bob always gets his hot dog plain. Can you imagine? He says all that relish and stuff gives him peptic ulcers. I'm sure Janet never gives him peptic ulcers, right? Ha-ha. Which reminds me . . . I've been meaning to let you all know that I'm thinking of taking some time away from the PTA myself. I'm having something of a time of my own and I think it would be good for me to just . . . work on that. So, I'll just be leaving. Good luck with the egg rolls.

SHE'S NOT THERE
Ali MacLean

Dramatic
ROB, 30

ROB's *depressed girlfriend,* ANNA, *has told him that she is leaving him.*

ROB   You don't think what you go through causes me pain? You don't think I can feel sadness? No? No. And you can't feel happiness the way I do. So, we both have something the other doesn't. But at least I try to understand what you are going through. Can you just try to be happy? I dare you to try that. I dare you to not wallow in this misery that you wear like a fucking costume. I dare you to try to get better. You want to "sleep forever"? You'll get that eventually. Everybody does. But what kind of ungrateful girl wants to sleep forever when others don't have a choice? You have a choice. You can wake up and go for a walk on the High Line, or order noodles from Hunan Palace, or just wake up and do nothing. Stay in bed all day. Listen to records with me. I'm not saying living with this cloud hanging over your head isn't hell. And I'm not saying the hard stuff is easy to tackle. Taxes, creditors, heartbreak, disappointment, failure. It sucks. But the shitty stuff is the price of admission. You get to be here on the planet. And there is always something that makes it worth it. I wake up every day no matter how bad shit in the world is because you are something worth waking up for. Stay awake Anna. Okay?

THE SHREW MUST GO ON
Lori M. Myers

Dramatic
KATHERINE, 30s–40s

KATHERINE *has traveled from Shakespeare's time to console a high school girl about to perform in* The Taming of the Shrew. *The backstage manager, an unruly sort, wants* KATHERINE *to leave and here,* KATHERINE *has had enough.*

KATHERINE   Yes, you fool-begged dullard. I'm still here and will continue to be here 'til the walls of this theater crumble and its nasty dust spread atop your monument so neither dormouse nor lizard will be able to read your despicable name on the stone beneath which you rest. Yes, I'm still here till time sheds your skin from your bones and crawls on its own fortitude to wrap itself around your meaty throat and strangle as you sputter and stutter even in death. I will be here, a grin on my face and in my heart as I replay your suffering and ignorance again and again from tyranny caused by my own tempestuous hands, hearing your shrill-shrieking screams echoing from the gates of hell. After all this time, from chattel and servant to suffragette and feminist. Why can't we seem to shed this massy baggage filled with doubt? When will we rise up to bide our truths and greet each morn not with puzzle, but with resolution? No more should we imprison ourselves within the dungeon of another's making, quell the shackles that wreak havoc on our souls, blot out the foes within ourselves who hinder and impede. We can. We must. Or else we are back to having shoeprints on our hands.

SKY CHEF
Cynthia Chapman

Dramatic
ROY WILBURS, 20, African American

ROY *is in the brig awaiting court martial proceedings on a United States Air Force base in New England during World War II. He is speaking to another black soldier, also in the brig.*

ROY   Look, it's my fault I didn't stop you. We're in the belly of the whale and I think I'm going to write a letter and someone's going to hunt down this whale and teach him a lesson, so he'll belch us up and set us free? You think I'm so smart, eh? Then what am I doing in this white man's army? No, I mean, I shouldn't be here. Look, I didn't volunteer. My number didn't "come up." Some white recruiters had my number all right. I told them I wanted to sign up for the Air Force ROTC while I was in school. They said sure, sign here. I signed my name with pride. Next thing I know, I'm drafted. Those sonofabitches had a good laugh at the stupid negro. I was so mad, so ashamed, I nearly left my wife and kid and fled to Canada. I wanted to forget that look in her eyes and I sure as hell didn't want them to get a piece of me. Yeah, Darlene has a lot to forgive while I'm here. I let her down and I can't fix it. So now, I'm here, and I gotta get something back for me, for us, and fight for something that makes sense, The Double V, you see?

SPLITTING INFINITY
Jamie Pachino

Dramatic
ROBBIE, 24

LEIGH SANGOLD, forty-nine, is a Nobel prize–winning astrophysicist whose post-doc student (with whom she's having an affair) has challenged her to prove God doesn't exist using physics. LEIGH flips his model on its head, instead. They should go after evidence of God through physics instead, together. Here, she tries to convince him.

ROBBIE   They all thought Einstein was a crank. They did. But eventually the entire community pointed to this twenty-six-year-old patent clerk and said That. You. Genius. Watson and Crick, the DNA model? You know what they said about how they figured it out? It was only after they threw away practically everything every other scientist had worked on that they created the model from which all of modern biology is based. Darwin knew what every other scientist of the day knew, but he thought what no one thought. What no one dared. Ever since the early twentieth century, it's been about the atom. Since they could pull it apart, that's all anyone wants to do. Photons, quarks, neutrinos, superstring, particles of particles, smaller and smaller. When what we should be doing is getting bigger—daring, dreaming—revoluting. Copernicus proved we weren't the center of the universe, and the plagues didn't come. Columbus went past the places on maps that said Here Be Dragons and nobody burned in a fiery death. Instead, we built America. We scaled Everest. Do you know what Edmund Hilary said after they reached the summit? He said: "we were relieved we found it." Because they didn't know where the top was—or if they'd ever find it. But they kept walking, because at the top was something no one had ever seen before. Something no one had dreamed. People used to seek out Everests. They don't anymore. Why? Why? . . . Because they think there aren't any left. You and I know they're wrong. *Don't we*?

SPLITTING INFINITY

Jamie Pachino

Dramatic
SAUL LIEBERMAN, 49

SAUL LIEBERMAN *is a rabbi who has been in love with his best friend, Nobel prize–winning* LEIGH SANGOLD, *since they met at ten years old. In their early twenties,* LEIGH *and* SAUL *came together romantically one night, but never again.* SAUL *has been carrying a torch for* LEIGH *ever since. It's Yom Kippur eve, the most holy night in the Jewish year.* SAUL *has finished his service at his shul and come to* LEIGH's *campus office, to tell her what has changed in his life.*

SAUL   Every week, fifteen hundred people sit in front of me and listen to what I have to say. Some are snoring, a few only show up for the High Holidays, but the rest come looking for the magic formula of how being good, plus doing good, plus knowing good and passing it on, might lead to their salvation. Or, at least ward off the bad juju for another week. On weekdays they make appointments with my secretary and come to my office. Rabbi, they say, I've lost hope . . . Rabbi, I'm afraid . . . Rabbi, my child won't speak to me anymore, God has forsaken me . . . please Rabbi, give me the words to salve, to heal, to undo, reclaim, recover, rescue, redeem, deliver . . . to save me. Please un-scorch this life I'm leading that I didn't mean to lead. You know what I tell them? That's their job. That's the job of their life. (*Beat.*) Three months ago, on my forty-ninth birthday, I asked Deborah for a divorce. And tonight, the reason I wasn't here, the reason I didn't come right away when you texted me was . . . she said yes. (*Beat.*) Leigh. We all reach forty-nine and wonder. If we've done the wrong things. And how much time is left to fix them. And we all want a great, giant life. God grants us ten days to make up for everything we've done. Isn't that the most remarkable thing? We're given the chance, every year, to name the things we did wrong, and change our lives. Well, I look at the sky still and ask for things, Leigh. Big things you think people don't look for anymore. And I've never stopped feeling the way I felt that night in the telescope with you. Neither have you. So, I'll be the one to say it. I'll be the one after all this time. Deborah said yes. And I don't want to wake up at fifty-nine or sixty-nine, or ninety-nine, in the middle of a life I didn't mean to lead. Look at me. Leigh. Look at me.

STRAIT OF GIBRALTAR
Andrea Lepcio

Dramatic
SAMEER, late 20s

SAMEER is speaking to MIRIAM, *his girlfriend. He wants to bring his sister* AMINA *from Morocco and asks* MIRIAM *to open a bank account for him in her name. He doesn't realize this is illegal.*

SAMEER   I don't want your money. No. But I could use help with. My father gave Amina cash to send to me for the business. She takes care of such things for him. And I have made money selling phones. But I have no account here, of course, because I am not legal. But sometimes to have an account would be useful. To put this money into an account at a bank. Could you open such an account? She will have a tourist visa to start. But it is difficult to have cash only cash. Denise can't help because. I don't understand everything. But she is a student and has financial aid and so she cannot take money. So, we were wondering if you could put our money in an account. With a plastic card. If I could have to pay for things. Like her ticket. It looks suspicious to buy with cash. To buy one way. I must pay with a credit card. Round trip. But it's not just the ticket. I mean, yes, you could get the ticket, okay, and I could give you the money. But, beside that, I need also to give you money to put in an account for the business. Your account. I need. Could you?

THE SUBSTITUTE TEACHER'S TALE

C. Denby Swanson

Comic
STUDENT, teens

A high school STUDENT who is not prepared for the final exam is questioned by the regular teacher's substitute.

STUDENT   My favorite Canterbury Tale is—uh—The Optometrist's Tale. It's one of the Tales that no one tells a lot. That's why you haven't heard of it, it's rare for subs to know it, it's like rare. But it was Mrs. C's favorite, yeah, totally it was her favorite. That's why it's my favorite too. It's these people, The Prioress, the Wife Who Took A Bath, the Pardoner, the Nun, the Second Nun, and this dude named Monk, like that TV show about the cop—they're pilgrims. Not like Thanksgiving, but like travelers. They're a group of travelers, they're like on a bus, they all get on this bus. And they all have the Bubonic Plague. So, they're on their way to the Optometrist. They're all going to an Optometrist because the Plague messes with your eyes. Like Mrs. Catley's eyes, her eyes are bad and she has a headache and she's missing school today and missing her own final exam I mean who does that? I bet you didn't know any of this—right? Good. Good. Yeah. So, let me just say that the bus is driven by a guy named Knight. Cuz—his dad, I guess. Was named Knight. And these pilgrims uh travelers, like they all have headaches too. Cuz they have the Plague. So, they get on this bus. And the bus is a local. It makes a lot of stops. And it's rush hour. So, they start talking to each other because why would anyone talk to strangers on the bus, I mean right? So, they go on this bus to the Optometrist, who has this little office like in a Costco. Which in Middle English was called, like the general store or whatever. And the Optometrist measures everybody's eyes and is like, you need new glasses and you need new glasses and you need new glasses. Like Oprah. And the Optometrist puts those little drops in their eyes and blows the puff of smoke to test for glaucoma—my grandmother had it so that's how I know what they do, it doesn't hurt it just feels weird like this little itty bitty tiny person in the machine just like FOOF right in your eye—and you know if Mrs. Catley went to the optometrist I bet they'd find that her eyesight is just a little bit worse each year because of all the terrible papers she makes us write, so that's also giving her a headache, and the Plague too, so definitely it's her own fault that she's out today. In any case, they all get new glasses and the Optometrist is like, Bye, see you next year if you don't die. And that's the Optometrist's Tale. So yeah. You can just leave Mrs. C a note that I passed the final because I really knew my tales.

THIN WALLS
Alice Eve Cohen

Dramatic
JANET, 45

JANET *is shy, quiet and demure, but when she starts talking, she has trouble stopping. Dedicated to her family, she has a strong sense of ethics and a passionate commitment to social justice. JANET's downstairs neighbor has invited her over to have coffee and to discuss a crisis facing the building's residents. It's the first time they've had a one-on-one visit, though JANET's teenage son regularly babysits for her neighbor's daughter. They live in a century-old building in New York City, once an elegant hotel, now a run-down low-income residential hotel with an eclectic array of residents. JANET and her husband ARNOLD have lived in the building for twenty-five years and have raised their two boys here.*

JANET   Well, as a matter of fact, I do have a hobby—you're probably too young to remember this, but um, in the sixties there was a television show called *The Fugitive*. Well, I just loved it in the sixties, and I love it now, and as a matter of fact I am a charter member of The Fugitive Fan Club. It's an international organization, we got a new member from the Netherlands last week. I edit the newsletter, we have an annual meeting in California. As a matter of fact, you might be interested in The Fugitive Fan Club, I could introduce you to some of the original people—of course most of the original producers and artists are either retired or dead, but . . . I get so carried away when I talk about this. You see, it's more than a hobby. It's an obsession. Could we change the subject? . . . What do I think about it? I feel exactly split down the middle. On the one hand, every liberal fiber of my being says if there are homeless people who need homes, and if this building has homes for fifty homeless families, well then give those people homes. But then the other part of me says that's na-ive, and I think about how ill-founded this plan is, and I think it would be a catastrophe. Look at the logic or the lack there-of. Most of the people who live in this building are living on the borderline of poverty to begin with. And so to oust those people to make room for the homeless simply creates a new population of homeless. And then speaking as a mother, I would be deluding myself to think anything other than that to turn this building into a homeless shelter, the building would become rife with violence and with substance abuse. You know, Arnold and I have lived in this building for the past two and a half decades, and we have seen this place change, we have seen the evolution of culture and society. But it is evolutionary change, and to impose such a sudden, radical and huge influx of a distressed and alien popula-tion—well, it would destroy the delicate fabric that holds this community together, this place that we consider in our wildest dreams to be some kind of an urban utopia, and we the homesteaders, the pioneers in it. And so, the bottom line is, if the city plan goes through, much as it breaks my heart to say this, my family will have to move.

THIN WALLS
Alice Eve Cohen

Seriocomic
HAVA, 23

HAVA *is an Israeli cellist, a talented graduate student studying at Juilliard. She is both tough and vulnerable. It's late at night. She's talking to her roommate, a thirty-six-year-old single mom, whose young daughter* HAVA *often babysits for. Neither of them has much money.* HAVA *has lived in this apartment for two years, in a century-old building in New York City; once an elegant hotel, it's now a run-down low-income residential hotel with an eclectic array of residents.* HAVA*'s family is in Israel and she misses them.*

HAVA   Oh, about the rent check, please wait maybe two days
before you deposit it, so that it will not bounce . . . again.
Could I talk to you about something? It's about my boyfriend. I think he is not trustable. Well, last week it was my
birthday, but it was not a happy birthday. My boyfriend did
not buy for me a present, so I said, it's my birthday, buy for
me a present, so he did, but it didn't mean anything because I had to tell him to buy it. My boyfriend is very plump
and soft. It feels so good. And so, a few nights ago we were
lying in bed, and I had my arm around him—and actually,
his breasts are bigger than mine, and I was fondling his soft
breasts and he jumped out of the bed and said "Stop that!
Don't ever touch me there again! You are humiliating me!"
And I said, "but you feel so good, I love to touch you there,"
and he said, "Don't! It's terrible!" and I said, "but it's just funny.
I am always complaining my breasts are too small, and you
think your breasts are too big, so it's funny." But he never
laughs from my jokes. My friends laugh from my jokes. I
think I am so funny. I am so cute. I am so nice. But I think
he doesn't love me. And then two nights ago we were at

his house watching a movie together. It was nice watching a movie. It was pornographic movie, but it was nice. And after the pornographic movie was over he says, "I don't want you to know where I keep the pornographic movie." So he goes into his room. In his room he has only one bed and one box. And I hear the box open and close, so I know the pornographic movie is in the box. So, he came out and I said, "I know the pornographic movie is in the box." And he said, "Never open the box." The next morning, we woke up and he had to go early to school. And if you say to somebody "don't open the box," she has to open the box. So, I opened the box. And inside there are fifty pornographic movies. And I think, "Why does he need fifty pornographic movies? And most of them are of two women. And I think, "Am I not enough?" And I think maybe I am for him just sex machine. You are the only person in all of New York I can talk to about this. Maybe because my family is in Israel, you are for me like a big sister. You are my big sister. I can respect and trust you. In all of New York City you are my only real friend. I didn't tell you this, but I had last month opportunity to share a very nice apartment one block from school. And I thought of it, but decided I would rather stay here with you, because even though you are very busy and I am very busy and you are often asleep when I come home, it is important for me to know that you are only on the other side of a thin wall.

THIN WALLS
Alice Eve Cohen

Seriocomic
MADY, 60

MADY is an angry, foul-mouthed woman with a smoker's cough. Her late husband JOE was a small-time drug dealer and loan shark, whom she screamed at day and night till his sudden death two years earlier. For twenty years, she lived with JOE in this windowless single room in a low-income residential hotel; they raised their two kids here. She's been lonely since JOE died and keeps her door open all the time. After a coughing fit, she talks to her next-door neighbor, who just happens to pass by MADY's open door.

MADY   I'm scared to death. Do you hear what I'm saying to you? I am scared to death. Can you believe it's two years since Joe died? Never forgive myself. Never forgive myself. If I hadn't a been so stupid, Joe would be here with me today. But I had to wait an hour for Joe Junior to arrive. Do you realize Joe was alive when the ambulance came for him? But he never made it to the hospital. Never forgive myself. Do you realize that I coulda had Joe buried for free in the veteran's cemetery? But I couldn't decide what to do and so I missed the deadline! The only thing left was cremation. So, they cremated Joe. Do you realize I coulda had Joe's ashes put for free in the veteran's mausoleum? But I couldn't make up my mind, and so I MISSED THE DEADLINE! So, they gave Joe's ashes to me. I didn't want Joe's ashes. What was I gonna do? I couldn't throw them away. So, I turned this place into a shrine to Joe. Everything's the same way it was two years ago. Joe's clothes hangin' in the same place they was two years ago. I put the vase with Joe's ashes on top of the TV set, so I knew I'd be lookin' at it all day long.

(Looking around the room.)

Used to say to Joe, "Get me outta this cave, Joe, ain't no windows here. Get me outta this cave. Get me outa this cave." When Joe died, the landlord told me if I took Joe's night shift, he'd get me a larger apartment. Never thought he'd do it. Can you believe, tomorrow I am movin' upstairs into a three-room apartment? Huge! What am I gonna do with all that space? I ain't got no furniture! My kids don't stay with me no more, place is too big for one person. And the noise and the light. I work all night, I sleep all day, I ain't never gonna sleep no more. People talk to me about a sunny day, a rainy day, a cloudy day. Don't mean nothin' to me. I ain't seen the day for twenty years. The bedroom. The bedroom, it's got two huge windows, I ain't never gonna be able to cut out all that light. And the noise from the—And the living room. The living room, it's a, it's a, it's a whatchamacallit. It's a, it's a fuckin' octagon! There's windows on all sides, it's great for plants! Do you understand what I am saying to you? I have been living in the darkness for twenty years. And tomorrow I move into the light. And I don't know *how* I'm gonna survive.

THIN WALLS
Alice Eve Cohen

Seriocomic
ARNOLD, 50

ARNOLD *is a friendly, gregarious, exuberant one-time hippie turned banker. He is visiting at the sunny apartment of his downstairs neighbor, a single mom whose daughter* ARNOLD*'s son used to babysit for.* ARNOLD *has heard through the grapevine that she is apartment-hunting, and he has dropped by to chat. They live in a century-old building in New York City, once an elegant hotel, now a run-down low-income residential hotel with an eclectic array of residents.* ARNOLD *and his wife* JANET *have lived in the building for twenty-five years.*

ARNOLD   At this juncture, I should mention that should you ever decide to move, the instant you leave you become part of the uh history and folklore of the building, and henceforth fair game for my uh storytelling. Which reminds me of a story. I love this story. This took place in your apartment, right here, apartment 303. This was during our tenure here so it was, let's see, uh, we'd been living here a few years, so this was uh 1970, 1972. Circus was in town. Circus left town. Couple of the performers defected and moved here into apartment 303. The fat lady and the dwarf. They were an item.

(He tries to stifle a laugh, covers his face to regain control.)

Now I'm gonna try not to laugh because that would be wrong.

(Clears throat, still stifling laughter.)

Well, the thing is, there were rumors that they were having an S and M relationship of some sort. They said she liked to bounce him off the walls. I lived right upstairs, I could hear everything. Anyway, every night he'd go to the bar across the street to get a couple of drinks. That restaurant on the corner, in the 1970s it was an uh Irish bar, McClanahan's or something like—anyway, he'd come back kind of loaded, walk in here. The minute the door closed this place sounded like a bowling alley.

(*Stifles his laughter.*)

But the point I'm trying to make. The point I'm tr—the point I'm trying to make is that the fat lady and the dwarf chose this place as home, because they felt at home here, because this place is the only place in the world, and we have traveled, and I believe this is the only place in the world that is soooo embracing—this is the reason I will probably live here happily until the day I die—this is the only place in the world where everybody can fit in.

THIS WILL BE OUR YEAR
Ali Maclean

Comic
HUGO, late 30s

HUGO, *a British rock star in the middle of a downward spiral, stands in the stage doorway talking to someone unseen (out to the audience).*

HUGO   How do you get backstage? I heard Keith Richards said you had to be important, talented, or fuckable. I don't know if I'm all three, but I'm here anyway. But, Honey, let me tell you something. You gotta stop thinking that backstage is some sort of Oz-like place where free money and love is handed out. You poor girls work so hard to get back here and it breaks my heart a little. I don't even want to know what Larry or the road crew made you do. Whatever you did for it, I'm not worth it. I'm telling you, I'm shite. What do you really think happens back there? It's boring. It's a cinderblock room with a formica card table. There's a bucket of beer and water and some shit-wilted catering trays. Some cum-stained futons. The label people are all crammed in there and they want to party. The A and R people are there with a thousand laminates around their necks, the prats. And we're exhausted and all we want to do is go back to the bloody hotel. But these tossers make us do this dog and pony show. Trot us out in front of these morning DJs in horrid flammable bowling shirts to smile for pictures with their scarecrow wives. And then there's the lot of you with your homemade tee shirts and glitter on your faces. How old are you? How many hours did you spend on this poster? How many hours do you spend thinking about me? Know how much time I'll spend thinking on you if we fuck? None. I won't even be thinking of you while I come. It's true. Cause I'm an arsehole. I really am. I'm a crap human being. How can you listen to all that and still want to shag me? That's pathetic. Know why I write songs? 'Cause I can't say what I mean to the people I love. It's true. The band all hate me. My ex-wife hates me. My own kids don't even remember what I look like. And I disappoint the person I love the most. You should be more selective of who you fuck. You don't want to be with me. "Hugo Turner" is a myth. And you're gonna be highly disappointed with the reality. I can destroy your life in record time. Seriously, they named a hurricane after me. So, I think you should go home before we make a really bad decision. Oh, I know. Bad decisions are sexy, aren't they? Until you get hurt. And believe me, you will be the one to get hurt. Not me. Because I don't feel fucking anything anymore. So, thanks for the brownies and all the blow, but really, you don't want this. You seem like a sweet girl. And you're very, very pretty. But, honestly, you're really, really fucked up. And I'll just fuck you up more.

TV IN MY BONES
C.S. Hanson

Comic
CECILIA, 30

The play begins with a "Prologue," as our narrator warms up the audience and sets up the show. Suddenly, CECILIA, a TV addict, comes out of the audience, onto the stage, to tell the narrator about her experience as a binge watcher. She is in search of something real and she becomes part of the show.

CECILIA   When I was bullied, TV was my friend. When I dreamed of moving to New York, TV was my friend. When I feared being homeless, TV was my friend. When we split, TV was my friend. When I had a cold and stayed home, TV was my friend. When I started online dating, TV was my friend. When he broke my heart, TV was my friend. When I broke his heart, TV was my friend. When I postponed that trip to Paris, TV was my friend. When the music stopped and everyone went home, TV was my friend. I streamed. I binge watched. I consumed new content. *Game of Thrones. Sherlock. House Of Cards. Fargo. Freaks and Geeks* and *Narcos* and *Mr. Robot* and *Breaking Bad* and *Homeland* and *Crazy Ex-Girlfriend* and . . . And then I stopped. I stopped watching. And now I wait. I wait for the next story. I wait for the moment when I will feel something as real as what I felt when I watched TV. I wait to meet someone who will love me the way Mark Harmon loved me every time I watched *NCIS*. I wait for friends, lovers, roommates, children, grandchildren, mom and dad. I wait because, I know, it's worth waiting for . . . I'm Cecilia. I'm searching for something real.

TWENTIETH CENTURY BLUES
Susan Miller

Dramatic
SIMON, late 20s to mid-30s

SIMON *has just returned from an aborted trip to meet his birth mother for the first time. He is telling his own mother what happened to change his mind.* NANI *is his grandmother who resides in an elder living facility.*

SIMON   I went to see Nani on my way out of town. When I got there, she was packing up her clothes. In a garbage bag. I tried to distract her. So, I took her on a mental tour of the old house on Taft Street. (*Beat.*) We walked through the whole house. (*Beat.*) I told her Zayda was playing the violin in the garage. Then we went into the family room. She seemed happy to be there. I named every book on the shelves practically. Will and Ariel Durant. *The History of the Jews. Watercolor Painting.* Arthur Miller's *Collected Plays.* We opened the big dictionary to look up words. Words she taught me. And then, the kitchen. Where we played Parchesi. The kitchen brought up the time she wouldn't make me macaroni and cheese and I took the pot in protest and left the house. She always tells that story. When we got to her bedroom, she looked like she could actually picture it. It seemed like she was sinking into the bed. Like she was finally home. I asked her what she remembered. And she just looked at me and said, *I remember everything.* (*Beat.*) But, after I left her and got to Pennsylvania, I just wanted to turn around. Nani knows me. She still knows who I am. As long as that's true, how can I go on this . . . self-indulgent odyssey to find everything that makes me someone else? (*Beat.*) How can I do that to *you*?

USHUAIA BLUE
Caridad Svich

Dramatic
PEPA (40s–50s)

PEPA *speaks to* SARA. PEPA *is native to Ushuaia, Argentina. She works in a lighthouse. The person to whom she is speaking is SARA, who is a filmmaker and research scientist who is visiting Ushuaia, Argentina, and is doing research. The context of the speech is within a conversation they are having about what to prioritize in the age of climate grief and change.*

PEPA   Why do we need so much? Why do we need so many things? I see them. The tourists with their . . . this phone and that phone and this device and the other, and always with an eye elsewhere—like what they have is not enough. When what they have could feed a small village. Sometimes the noise is like a sickness. This noise of suffering. And I think we will drown in this ridiculous noise. Because we will not know what else to do. But then I remember this thing that happens sometimes when I wake up from a terrible sleep. I put my feet on the ground, and it is cold because I have forgotten my slippers, and oh, how my feet shiver. Like the hurt of the earth itself. And I want to curse at everything. Use all the beautiful terrible words in all of the languages. But I don't. I let my feet find their warmth. I let them not give in to the cold. And as soon as I do, my whole body is thinking of hopeful things. Even though it knows somewhere there is massive stupidity and greed and power and hate. I take a step. I look out. I think—I will not let myself understand where I am. I will not let myself know too much. Because it is only when I say I do not know … that maybe some true knowing comes through.

A VERY PRESENT PRESENCE

Ann Timmons

Dramatic
ALICE, late 40s

ALICE, mother, wife, and career woman who, having done everything "right," is now at a crossroads in her life. She has fled from her home, husband, and two twenty-something children to the farmhouse to "figure things out." Her plans are interrupted by a visitation from the "presence" of her Great-Aunt NELL, who died in 1935. NELL, appointed as ALICE's guide from the Other Side, has not yet been successful at that. But she has managed to annoy ALICE a great deal.

ALICE   Alright! ALRIGHT! Oh my God! What am I doing?? Here I am, screaming at a . . . a … It's the very definition of crazy! I need to . . . It will be all right. Focus. Breathe into the center. Relax.

(Closes eyes. Breathes deeply. Pause. Opens eyes. Sees NELL.)

GET OUT! GET OUT! Get out of my head! Get out of my house! Go away and leave me alone. Stop haunting me! *(Silence.)* Oh, are you stuck? Serves you right! *(Pause.)* Ah! What's that sound? Nothing. Oh, wait! It's the sound of my own thoughts. That's what I came up here for. Quiet! Not the delusional ramblings of some batty old ghost who probably doesn't even exist. *(Pause.)* You've got a lot of nerve! Telling me about my childhood. How Grammie raised us. I was there. You weren't! Of course, she loved us! She fed us and clothed us and protected us. Why would she have done that if not for love, huh? *(Pause.)* Everything I know I know because she taught me. She . . . she showed me how to fold tee shirts so they fit in the drawer. Because you don't want them just flopping around in there. She taught me the correct way to do things! Everything. She had standards. She set me an example: how to be organized and capable and get it right the first time and OH MY GOD! I see it now! (*Pause.*) Grammie taught me how to make my life look perfect on the outside but . . . not how to fill it on the inside. It was appearances that mattered. (*Pause.*) No wonder Mom got out!

VICTORIA AND HENRY
T. Cat Ford

Dramatic
VICTORIA WOODHULL, 30s–40s

VICTORIA WOODHULL, *a spiritualist and proponent of the free love movement, begs* HENRY WARD BEECHER *to join her in the fight for sexual equality.*

VICTORIA   How many men are unfaithful to their wives? How many women remain with their husbands because they have no other means of support? The poor young woman who is a Christian believes she can escape hell only by obeying St. Paul's injunction that wives should submit to their husbands. Think of it! I say damn such Christianity as that. You, sir, preach the gospel of love but . . . is your wife, the woman you call "The Griffin," a happy woman? Has her marriage been a blessing to her? And, if not, we must ask why for her good! For her happiness, if such a thing is possible. You do not know what I have seen. What I have heard. We must destroy this sham morality under which we live and under which some of us die. Women die at the hands of frustrated husbands. Men's souls wither from lying to their wives and then lying with women who are not their wives. Children . . . children . . . have you seen my son? My poor, imbecile . . . all that I am I have become through sorrow. Have you truly looked into the eyes of a woman who has been abused for the sake of her sex? Look into my eyes . . . abused women are not whole. We cannot produce proper children. The sins of the father. The sins of the father. You love your daughters, don't you? Would you have men treat them as you treat your many lovers? Would you have your daughters treated as you treat their mother? You preach the gospel of love—now live it! We can be free. We will be free. This is our moment. Oh, can you feel it?

(*Referring to the spirits who she feels are now surrounding her.*)

We are not alone. Oh, oh, I can hear them, my voices, my spirits! They are telling me . . . you and I are meant to lead a revolution! We will free women and men from the sexual slavery that has held us in thrall for millennia. Think of it. Living free to love those around us in true equality and joy. Victory for truth! For anyone who lives not in truth but in lie, lives in suffering. We will start a campaign! You and I speaking together for the cause will be unstoppable. Mrs. Stanton and Miss Anthony think they can affect change by gaining the vote. How absurd. True sexual equality begins in bed.

VULCANIC SURRENDER
J. Lois Diamond

Dramatic
JEANINE, mid-30s

JEANINE, *a nurse, is speaking to her best friend* TIM, *a forty-year-old drag queen, who is a little rough around the edges. They are in a piano bar in the West Village on Halloween, 1993.* TIM *loves surface glamour but eventually learns to confide his deep dark secret to his one true friend, while she attempts to help him overcome his addictions. As part of that strategy, she shares a drug experience she once had.*

JEANINE   I tried opiates once. Morphine. I had access to the pharmaceuticals and I did thirty milligrams of morphine. I ingested it. And it was good. Dare I say that it was wonderful. I was going through a lot. I was getting over a break-up, my father had recently died, and I was so depressed. But for that hour, I felt the most profound joy I have every felt in my entire life. I remember thinking, now I know why they shoot heroin. All those emaciated twitching bodies in the emergency room had seen ecstasy! I was so euphoric. It was like, all my problems were still there, but I didn't care. I would think about them, and laugh! Isn't that strange?! It was like for once, everything was really OK, completely OK. I realized how fragmented I usually am. How I worry each night about everything I've said and done that day, who I've offended, and who's offended me, and the list is always endless. My mind never rests. It ticks like a metronome, hanging on to this obsession or that fear, but on morphine, there was this glorious moment of silence. I was as close to God as I'll ever be.

WAR ORPHAN

Shellen Lubin

Dramatic
JEFF, 32

JEFF, a gay man, has made a case to his parents that he and his best friend SUSAN are getting married so they can be each other's family and make a family together, but the real reason is so that they will be forced to produce his birth certificate, and he can find out the truth about whether or not he was adopted.

JEFF   I was giving that whole song and dance to my mother, again, about why we were going to get married, and as I was telling her, I was also listening to myself. And, Susan, I know on one level this sounds really stupid—because I am most definitely gay and I don't believe I will ever again have a sexual relationship with a woman—the inherent bi-sexual nature of all human beings notwithstanding—but on another level, everything I was saying made too much sense. I should marry you—if those were really the reasons I was doing it, which they're not. I mean, we do know each other so well and love each other so much and we do both want a family and we do both fall in love with the worst possible people— yes, both of us. You do, too, you know it. And you are the most consistent and meaningful relationship in my life. And, I know I'm not an actor, but maybe it's something like what happens to actors when they're playing a part that's more true than they are themselves, but I was so completely there in what I was saying and I was so aware of how right it was, that it made me realize that if everything I said was true but that wasn't really the reason I was doing it, then I was even more of a mess than I thought.

WAR ORPHAN
Shellen Lubin

Dramatic
JEFF, 32

JEFF, a gay man, tries to explain to his mother why he hated being a Psychologist and gave up on that career, even though it afforded him money and prestige and a much easier life.

JEFF   I don't like most people. When I thought about being a therapist, I thought about how other people felt, how I could help them with what they were going through. But I didn't realize how I would feel about them. My life is how I feel about what I'm doing, so if they're my clients, that's my life. Mom, for the last couple of years I would come home every night tirading about what self-involved, narcissistic, petulant infants my clients were. Their problems seemed about as profound to me as those of a lima bean. And by these last few months, all I wanted to do, every minute, was yell at them: "Grow up. Get a life. Care about something. Other than yourself. Why don't you see how easy you've got it? Do something important. Do something valuable in the world. Just do something. Anything." I sat there and nodded sympathetically and asked "the right questions" so that they could make their little discoveries once every three months about how some adult—fill in the blank—mother, father, uncle, teacher, babysitter—had done some detestable thing to them—fill in the blank—rape, rage, alcohol, neglect—and feel smug and sanctimonious that they had an absolute right—not to get healthy and responsible and mature, mind you, they never wanted that—but an absolute right to be as miserable and selfish as they were.

WAR ORPHAN
Shellen Lubin

Dramatic
JEFF, 32

JEFF, *a gay man, is reeling from a brief but passionate fling with a very beautiful, very intelligent, extremely manipulative and dishonest man. This is the first time since the breakup that he has spoken to his best friend, SUSAN, who introduced the two of them.*

JEFF   That night, after I first went home with him? I knew I was potentially in serious trouble. I mean, apart from the fact that he is exceptionally gorgeous and even more exceptionally— wickedly—bright, he was also seriously taken with me. You don't know how difficult it is to keep any kind of healthy perspective on anything in the face of that. So, here's what I did. I took my jar of marbles out of the closet—you know, the box of toys and stuff I'm saving for Bob and Michelle's to-be-kids—and I set that jar out next to the clear glass bowl on the shelf over the stereo, and I took one marble out of that jar and put it in that clear glass bowl for his telling me that he didn't have any plans that Sunday, when he was supposed to be meeting you. And then I said out loud to anyone who was around to hear—which of course no one was because my roommate works weekends—I said every time I catch him in a lie—not suspect, but actually am one hundred percent positively sure that he has lied to me, not even to anyone else—about anything, though, absolutely anything—one marble goes from that jar into that clear glass bowl. And in only three short weeks, that is 5:00 p.m. yesterday when he told me he had to go out for a while to bring chicken soup to his sick friend Joe Kandrovsky, and his extremely fine friend Joe Kandrovsky called while he was gone and left a message on his machine that said, basically, that they hadn't spoken in a week, I left, before he came back, and came home and took the last marble—yes, the very last marble—out of the jar that was once oh-so-full of marbles, and put it into the bowl. And the bowl, the clear glass bowl? Well, you can't see any clear glass anymore, you know what I mean? Nothing's clear anymore. Except that.

WHAT WOULD JESUS DO?

Yvette Heyliger

Dramatic
JOHN WILSON, SR., early 50s, African American

An upstanding, church-going husband and father has exposed his wife to HIV. This confession is delivered to the congregation of the Open Bible Church for Healing, Spiritual Renewal, and Deliverance.

WILSON   Church, I have forsaken my loving wife of twenty years—this wonderful woman of God who has served you so well today. "A virtuous woman is a crown to her husband . . ." but I . . . I committed adultery! I cheated on my best friend and partner, the mother of my children. I took her life into my hands through my actions and that is why she must get tested. I have no explanation for my actions. It wasn't something that was planned. I didn't go looking for trouble. It just happened! God help me, it just happened. There are men who meet in the park, at a certain place, after dark. I stumbled on it one night when I was out for a run. What I beheld—I couldn't believe! What the Bible talks about— right before my eyes! "And likewise, also the men, leaving the natural use of the woman, burned in their lust one toward another; men with men working that which is unseemly, and receiving in themselves that recompense of their error which was meet." I wanted to curse them, but I couldn't . . . I wanted to shut my eyes, but I couldn't . . . I wanted to run away, but I couldn't! My feet were held fast to that spot. My face felt flushed, my palms were sweaty, my stomach was doing flip flops. I was ablaze, burning in the heat of unsolicited desire! It was like I had no control over how my . . . member . . . was reacting. The next time I went out for a run, I couldn't stop my feet from moving to that place, and before I knew it, I was there—participating! I don't know why I felt drawn to have sex with a man. I don't know why. I just . . . wasn't thinking! It's like I was in a . . . a trance . . . or something. Like it wasn't really happening—but it was! "I delight in the law of God after the inward man; but I see another law in my members, warring against the law of my mind and bringing me into captivity to the law of sin . . . O wretched man that I am! Who shall deliver me . . . who shall deliver me from the body of this death?" I prayed, and prayed and prayed for God to take away this burden, but it doesn't go away! Do you think that I liked that this happened? That I wanted it to happen? No! I am ashamed; ashamed that I had the desire, ashamed that I liked it. I knew what I was doing was wrong—but it felt right. God help me, it felt right! I know what the Bible says! I am just as shocked as my family is, as you are! I hear the way some of you Bible-totin', scripture quotin' folks talk. You view homosexuality as a curse against a race with too many strikes already against it. The guilt is unbearable. It's like you're letting down black women, the black community, black history, black pride, the black church, the whole black race!

WHEN NIGHT FALLS
Cynthia Grace Robinson

Dramatic
GEORGE, 50s

GEORGE *speaks to his wife as he stands in the bedroom of their daughter, EVE, who has recently passed away.*

GEORGE   All the stuff I haul around in that truck. Out there. It belonged to somebody. Once. Somewhere. I'll never know the people or their stories, but each and every item has a history behind it. They just call me to come and collect what's cluttering up their rooms and their closets and their basements. Most of the time it's junk. Shoot, half the time I make a stop at the junkyard and dump it myself. It's just garbage, right? Just things. But the other half of the time there's somethin' in there of value. And it's my job to give it new life. It feels good to be able to do that. To extend a life by collecting someone's things. Eve. My beautiful Eve. My little baby girl is gone and all I have left are her things. Dolls. Dresses. Books. Pictures. Her angelic voice recorded on my phone. Letters. Her bike. Ribbons. Makeup. Jewelry. Shoes. Man, she has lots and lots of shoes. All her precious things. Things. Things. Things. That's all I got left of that beautiful girl's life. What the hell do I want with all these things? I ask myself—What can I do with them? Then I realize. I want to touch anything that she touched and I want to caress it. I wanna savor it. And I wanna smell it, hoping I'll feel something. Maybe I'll feel her breath on my face. Maybe I'll feel her heart beating in my chest. Maybe I'll hear her whispering in my ear once more. Maybe her things can give **me** new life. Maybe she'll live on in some small way. Yeah, maybe her things will resurrect her . . . for me . . . in me.

WHITE ASHES
Barbara Blatner

Dramatic
JOHN, 30s

JOHN, *longtime inmate of White Ash Psychiatric Hospital, says goodbye to his beloved ESTHER, another inmate who is leaving the hospital for good. John Lennon has recently been shot.*

JOHN   Hope springs eternal. Dopes, too. Oh yeah. And thanks, and merry holidays, nineteen-hundred-and-whatever-it-is-A.D., after drugs, after dinner, after Dwight D. Assenhower, in the year of our dreaming, gimme music. Brumm brumm. As I said to my old pal Elvis: Priscilla will come back, you wait and see. And now I hear Yoko's crying in her cups 'bout ole John, so I say: don't fret, old girl, you'll see him again. Be patient. Like I'm patient here in this shady hotel, patient with my mentality, mental in my carnality, for nigh on five or ten or fifteen or a hundred thousand years of unrecorded time. Hey, it's not the Poconos, but it's home, folks. Brumm brumm. Time here gives me so much time, it's no time at all. Brumm brumm. Yeah, Lennon, somebody got you, but I swear to god you're comin' back in the spring, like Jesus did. You're gonna rise outta the dead ground with the groundhogs. You watch, one a' these days, I'm gonna rise up, too. I'm gonna straighten it all out, like Esther's doin', out in the world o' time. Where the music goes on, brumm brumm. Music's everywhere, I say to John, no matter where you are, everywhere the music goes on. Nothin' can hold it back, not loneliness or space or time. Wherever you are, man, the music goes on. Brumm brumm. And on. Brumm. And on. Brumm brumm, brumm brumm . . .

THE WISH
Crystal Adaway

Dramatic
BARBARA, 50

BARBARA *is speaking to her adult daughters and her ex-husband on her birthday. None of the women have seen him since he left them all for a pretty young thing twelve years ago.* BARBARA's *younger daughter kidnapped him and trussed him to a chair as a birthday gift. Here,* BARBARA *reflects on the family's beginnings.*

BARBARA   Nobody talked about the important stuff back then, the things people should talk about, and come to terms with, before saying "I do." If you were in love, or what you thought was love, you got married. You listened to the preacher saying all those words about commitment and faith and death. But it's like buying a car, or . . . or the thing you have to check the box on in one of those dating sites: you scroll through it, not reading, not caring enough to understand what you're signing up for. You just want to get to what you think is the fun stuff, so you click on the "I agree" button and hope for the best. You work hard, buy a little house, have lots and lots of sex. Get a cross-eyed cat that likes to eat curtains. Get pregnant in five minutes. Get fat for nine months. Have a beautiful baby girl who smells like sunshine . . . (*Long beat.*) But she is always hungry, always crying, always needing to be changed, always awake, always needing, needing, needing something. Always needing me. My life is no longer my own. I'm exhausted, and nothing I do will soothe you. And your father is no help at all. You could've tried harder, Richard! I needed you. I know you felt put out, goddamnit. I know! You can't stand being second fiddle. Jesus Christ! For nearly four years, I had one baby or another latched to my body all day, every day, sucking the life out of me through cracked nipples. My body was no longer my own. It felt like a tool for everyone else. When they finally would sleep, I'd have my skin back for a blessed few hours. I couldn't give it to you. I needed it. (*Beat.*) But I hated it. Stretched and dry, flabby and red. I didn't recognize myself in the mirror. That was somebody else's ugly body. I didn't want to look at me, why would you want to?

WIT'S END
Christine Foster

Dramatic
DEIRDRE, 50

DEIRDRE, *a professional writer, has just met a dazzling young musician, her stepdaughter's boyfriend, and is struggling with her feelings. Here, she is addressing her Muse.*

DEIRDRE   What am I doing? Seriously. Why do I think it's my job to open their eyes, or give them a taste for truth and beauty? They are truth and beauty, for God's sake. What was it they used to write on steamer trunks? "Not Needed on This Voyage." That's me. And what do I need? To work. This should be the most productive time of my life. Instead I'm withering. Withering away. I stand on Withering Heights alone with my thoughts. None of which are particularly pleasant. What do you say, Muse? Mmmm? Out of earshot again? Or just on a mandatory union break? You really should come back, you know. If only to have a laugh. To hear my voice go all taut and strangled at the sight of a strong, young . . . neck. And you definitely shouldn't leave me alone with him. I don't know whether I want him to shut up, or never stop talking. I am "this close" to wanting to . . . impress him. How? I dunno. And what for? If you were here I could at least get some work done. I could focus. My mother used to say, "A real lady never hurries to please a man. That's for housemaids and hookers." Of course Mama never did know Thing One about pleasing herself. (*Beat.*) It's all right. I can do this. I can be Auntie Mame. The Wise Woman of the Woods. The Fairy Godmother. Super Crone. I'm doing okay. He is lovely, but I have brakes. Unfortunately, I have no reverse.

WOLVES AT THE DOOR
Ali MacLean

Dramatic
GAVIN, mid-40s

GAVIN, *whose stepdaughter was murdered in a mass shooting,*
explains to his wife GRACE *that he has been grieving, too.*

GAVIN   Jesus, Grace! All I've been doing is dealing with you!
Making sure you are okay. Tip-toeing around you. Not wanting to set you off. You sleep in ten-minute increments with
your fists balled up in attack mode. The slightest thing, like
a rustle of the pillow, wakes you. And when you are sleep
deprived, you're even more on edge, which is bad because
keeping your equilibrium steady is a high wire act these
days. I don't sleep next to you because *I* don't sleep, period! I
haven't since that day. I wake up every night in a cold sweat,
shaking, because I have this repeating nightmare about
how I could have stopped him. I should have been able to
keep her safe. It's my one job to keep the two of you safe.
And my mind plays it over and over in this evil Tetris battle
where I shift things to try to make it work. Tackling him to
the ground. Shoving her out of the way. Pulling out my own
gun and obliterating him. Taking the bullet for her. My head
tries to create this reality where I go all Die Hard on this piece
of shit and save her. But I wake up every time and nothing
is different. She's still gone, and you are shattered, and I
have failed you both. No matter how many times I play the
scenario out, no matter how many times I reset the game, I
lose. Every time I look at your face, I am reminded that I have
failed. I can't win. I can't win with you no matter what I do.
For the record? I fucking miss her too.

WOMAN DESCENDING A STAIRCASE
Phoebe Eaton

Dramatic
SYLVIA PLATH, 30

SYLVIA's estranged husband, faithless fellow poet TED HUGHES, has just left with their children for a visit to a nearby zoo. This evening, she will be attempting to win him back over dinner. This is direct address to the audience.

SYLVIA   I don't know how we can afford to be apart, Ted and me I mean there's
Assia Wevill's money I suppose. Ted knows how to pick 'em!
But I mean
She's married, too!
A minor detail
Well I hope that bitch can type
I typed that man's every coughed-up hairball
Over and over
Stamped and mailed them
Good luck and Godspeed
You know back in college, I was interned one summer in New York City at *Mademoiselle*
magazine
This is where I first understood I was equipped neither mentally nor physically to be
An obedient little-hat-wearing white-glove career girl
Fastest typist on the floor!
Well I'm sorry I mentioned it
So you want to be a writer?
Here, type some rejection letters. Over and over. Talk about *drudgery*. My fault for
bragging
Sitting there blah-di-blah-blah-ing the same old crap

"Dear Bitsy Berrigan, Dear Charlie Maynard,
We received your submission but it does not suit our editori-
al needs at present"
I was specifically instructed never to say
"We're sorry"
Never to say sorry
Because the mademoiselles of *Mademoiselle* magazine
weren't
sorry
So why pretend?
This made a powerful impression

(*To Ted, somewhere in the ether.*)

You weren't just touched by the wand, Ted Hughes
I made you. *I!*
You tell me that I cracked the window an inch
So you shot out like a mouse
Ted, this isn't East Germany, Ted
You can leave any time
He left that night
Some former friends of mine claim I am dictatorial!
"We'd come, but she doesn't want to," he'd tell them
"I'm getting the signal we should go now"
Throwing a look
Behind my back
Funspoiler
Killjoy
Just following orders, were you?
Somebody had to take the decision, call the shots
But I am, as ever, an optimist. Like everybody from my native
land
Staring that grinning sheep failure in the face and declaring
victory is what we do best.
Okay so we never got bombed, we had the luxury of
distance

But here it's whinging, excuses, and misdirection
All this time, you didn't taste what I am made of
Sea salt and vinegar
And now I'm back
In London!
Amongst intelligent people who don't just stand around like cattle
I will have important conversations about Dachau. *The Bomb!*
And I will beat you
I will out-money you!
I am at the Everest peak of my creative powers and I'm just thirty years on this planet.

WOMAN DESCENDING A STAIRCASE
Phoebe Eaton

Dramatic
SYLVIA PLATH, 30

SYLVIA *kills time awaiting the return of her children and her es-*
tranged faithless fellow poet husband TED HUGHES *from a nearby*
zoo. She teeters on the brink of self-destruction even as she plots
how to win him back. This is direct address to the audience.

SYLVIA   At *Mademoiselle* magazine, there was a home-
entertaining editor
Kitty McMann
Every winter Kitty busted out a gorgeous full-length mink
polo coat the color of whiskey
Anyway, it was left to me to call the man to come get it for
cold storage
A few of us were in the sample closet, trying it on
What luxury
I asked someone about Mr. McMann
Well there never was any Mr. McMann
Kitty thought she deserved a mink at her age. So she treated
herself
There was no *being grateful* like the other married ladies
There are people who feel grateful and others who feel
deserving
If you're a woman, they want you to be grateful even if
you've worked like
a sled dog
In harness since the Ice Age
So you pretend
Years ago, Kitty set her cap for some fellow, and when
that went nowhere
She never got over it

I do believe she drank
You can tell these things
I don't want to be the one who
can't get over it
I won't have to ever
get over *anything*
if I stop it from
happening
in the first place
Lord I wish I had
A sun tan
Ted's girl missed out on a tan
In Spain
I hear
They hardly left the room
She told people
Who told me
Because people are people
Enjoying the show through
Opera glasses
When I was in
high school, some of the other girls, the ones who
had Daddies, the Daddies who
had money
They would come back from Christmas, their faces the color
of iced tea
I envied them. I wanted
their lives as fast as humanly possible, and I wanted it all,
pronto
I need to write the smash-hit potboiler. That's where the
money is. I have one in me
That's been the plan
There's always a plan
And then I'll be off to Italy, which is superior to
scrubby, barren Spain in every way culturally

Poems were something I could write before my life hap-
pened yet
The problem is, now that life is happening, I think I may have
had
Too much
An overdose
Of reality

WOMAN DESCENDING A STAIRCASE
Phoebe Eaton

Dramatic
SYLVIA PLATH, 30

Just back from what she (mistakenly) believed would be a date with estranged philandering husband TED HUGHES, SYLVIA *has just put her signature to their divorce papers. This is direct address to the audience.*

SYLVIA   This divorce is underway!
A brick through a window showing
I. Mean. Business!
Listen
Sappho didn't have a man
Stranded there on the desert island of Lesbos
The greatest poetess of ancient times
Granted she had no pressing need for one
Lucky bitch (*Long pause.*)
Well perhaps it needs time to sink in. Perhaps my Ted's gone off to
Spain again, I don't understand—
—with everybody knowing? What he did to his wife and children?
There's no shame. None
I wonder. I wonder how he'd enjoy being *that* person
In the bell jar
Everybody staring, pointing
Like he's one of his favorite creatures over in the zoo there
Behind bars the rest of his days
For what he's gone and done. To us
Craving fame *as* much as I. Despite his mealy-mouthed protestations
How fast fame turns to infamy

Him driven mad by it! Mad as a stoat!
Yes
Quite
His owing me for all I'd done for him was his prison, I know he thought it
Now let him stay put away for all he did for *me*
"There goes that monster Ted Hughes. Wasn't it his wife who tried to—
Who—" (*Pause.*)
Now if you'll excuse me, I have to go
fix breakfast
for my family
Sliced bread and mugs of milk
They will be dining this morning in their cots
al fresco
The windows wide open, my two gorgeous baby bundles
All right, so yes, little Nicky still thinks cups are toys

Listen, he's a clever boy. I mean, look at his parents. He'll figure it out, and all right
the menu's not up to usual standards but it'll do. As a statement, an artistic
statement. It's how they'll know, everybody will know, *definitively*
In a matter of hours
Mommy cares. Mommy's not
crazy after all. Look!
She made *breakfast!*
She's not some crazy-bitch nut job who loses her holy mind and drowns her kittens like
she's Medea or something, I mean good golly. They'll see it in her work!
The best work of her life!
Okay, all right, so she's had those kinds of thoughts. Ghastly, clawing thoughts

But doesn't every mother? I mean really
Can we not kid ourselves here?
Those voices that drown out reason. Singing to her
ceaselessly
Calling her out to the cold numb sea, a child latched to each
arm
But terminally sane woman she is
There's a new day dawning, and on her father's dead body,
she swears
She is done listening

ZOOM BIRTHDAY PARTY
Saviana Stanescu

Comic
OANA, 20

*After a breakup with CHRIS, who left her for a "trust fund girl,"
OANA, a Romanian student at NYU, has a revenge fantasy in which
she turns into Countess Dracula (a feminist version of Count Dracula
re-imagined by herself), and punishes her ex-boyfriend.*

OANA   Commoner Chris—what are you doing here, in my
castle? (*Sexy tone.*) Wanna, wanna, wanna, wanna—? (*Tough
tone.*) Tough luck. Today I'm not in the mood for that. Do you
know who I am? I am Countess Dracula. No, I'm not Count
Dracula's wife. I'm not his bride, not his mistress, not his
mother. Count Dracula doesn't even exist. He was invented
by a white western man like you. A nice, charismatic, attractive man, like you. A progressive man. Like you. A lovely
man—who could also be a little selfish, insensitive, opportu-
nistic, cruel . . . patronizing, entitled, arrogant, jerk
. . . gold-digging muttafuckin' liar hypocrite asshole! Bad boy,
bad boy . . . What shall I do with you? Torture you? Nooo,
you might like it too much. Suck your blood? Nah. I'm not
turning you into a vampire. You don't deserve it. Impale you?
That would make some historical sense . . . Nope. It would
only confirm the stereotype. Turn you into a bat? No! This is
not a fucking fairytale. Or I could—Cut off your tongue, your
hands, your feet, your dick . . . Grip each eyeball, twist, and
pull until your eyes pop out of the socket . . . I could easily
kill you, or throw you to the famished wolves . . . But I don't
know . . . This is not the way I want to write this story . . .

RIGHTS AND PERMISSIONS

To obtain the entire text, contact the rights holder.